JACKIE MILBURN'S
NEWCASTLE UNITED
SCRAPBOOK

THE MILBURN FAMILY TREE

Jack Milburn (Northumberland)

Jack Milburn (Ashington)

Alec Milburn (Ashington)

Jackie Milburn
(Newcastle United & England)

Tanner Milburn (Ashington)

Bob Charlton—Cissie Milburn Jack
(Leeds)

George
(Leeds &
Chesterfield)

Jim
(Leeds)

Stan
(Chesterfield &
Leicester)

Jackie Charlton
(Leeds & England)

Bobby Charlton
(Manchester Utd. & England)

JACKIE MILBURN'S NEWCASTLE UNITED SCRAPBOOK

by
Jackie Milburn

PICTORIAL
PRESENTATIONS

SOUVENIR PRESS

I would like to place on record my thanks and appreciation to writer JOHN GIBSON for his invaluable help in putting this book together. John has been a black-and-white fanatic since birth and has been extremely closely involved with Newcastle United in a professional capacity for the last 15 years. He has helped gather up the threads of my thoughts and memories to knit them together into a story of pride and love about 'our Club.'

ACKNOWLEDGEMENTS

Jackie Milburn would like to thank the following for the use of photographs: Newcastle Chronicle and Journal Ltd, Daily Express, News of the World and R. L. Palmer.

First published 1981 by Souvenir Press Ltd,
43 Great Russell Street, London WC1B 3PA
and simultaneously in Canada

ISBN 0 285 62492 X
ISBN 0 285 62510 1

Filmset and printed in Great Britain by
BAS Printers Limited, Over Wallop, Hampshire

CONTENTS

MY LOVE AFFAIR

THE shrill of the final whistle set my spine tingling. Emotions flooded in. There was noise—deafening noise—and everywhere a sea of black and white. I felt exhausted and triumphant, elated and drained, all at the same time. Amid all the hullabaloo Stanley Matthews came across and grabbed me by the hand: 'Well done, Jackie,' he said. 'You deserved it. Well done.'

It was 28 April 1951, and the greatest day in my long love affair with Newcastle United. We had just won the FA Cup at Wembley, beating Blackpool 2–0 in what was supposed to have been the Matthews final. Anyone who didn't hail from Tyneside might have been forgiven for hoping Stan would at last walk away with that elusive Cupwinner's medal. But it wasn't to be. We beat them fair and square, and

JACKIE MILBURN shakes hands with Field Marshal Montgomery before a match at Bolton in 1949.

A forward line to be feared— Tommy Waker, Billy Foulkes, Jackie Milburn, George Robledo and Bobby Mitchell.

what's more, I scored both the goals.

What a marvellous, marvellous feeling it was. That great actor, Robert Newton summed it up beautifully when we met at the beginning of the following season. 'My boy,' he rasped, rolling those huge, expressive eyes, 'I would give that arm off by there' (striking his outstretched hand across his bicep) 'and that arm off by there to do what you did. Every actor who was ever born yearns to dominate the centre of the stage just once in his career with the whole world watching him and you did it twice in the one day!'

I lived by goals. You could say they were my stock in trade, yet these two were particularly satisfying because they gave me the chance to display contrasting skills. The more famous of the two became known as the 'backheel goal'. Tommy Walker, our outside-right, pushed the ball to little Ernie Taylor and as he did I yelled: 'Backheel it!' Ernie did but even so I was really too far over the ball. I struck it with all my might and from 28 yards it flew straight as an arrow into the back of the net. Had I been better positioned when I made contact it would probably have hit the crossbar.

But for me the goal that mattered was the other one. This was a goal for the connoisseur, the one every centre-forward dreams of scoring—real copy-book stuff. I remember starting my run from the halfway line, then running and running until I forced the goalkeeper, George Farm, to commit himself. Then all I had to do was tuck the ball home in the gap he had unwittingly opened up. I knew from the

moment the ball left my foot that I'd scored, and I turned away without even waiting to see the ball hit the back of the net.

The trouble with a free run like that is that you can't quite believe it's happening. You keep seeing imaginary shadows chasing you, and you're convinced you can feel the panting breath of half a dozen defenders down the back of your neck. That's why it means so much to score: so many things could go wrong.

I still look on the 1951 Cup Final as the high point of my years with Newcastle United. We were back at Wembley the following year when we won again, and we completed the hat-trick in 1955 when I scored the fastest goal in the history of the finals with a header after 45 seconds. But the '51 team was the best. We believed then as now that the black-and-white striped shirt of the Magpies was the finest a footballer could wear and the talent and spirit in that team was second to none. For a start we had Jack Fairbrother, a goalkeeper who was unbelievable on his angles; then there was huge Frank Brennan, and Bobby Cowell and Ernie Taylor, not forgetting my fellow goal-scorer George Robledo, or Mitch on the left wing. What was more, we had Joe Harvey as our skipper. It never mattered to Joe how much of a rollicking he got from the crowd: he made his own decisions and he knew his players were always 100 per cent behind

7

ABOVE: Jackie caught in mid-air as he smashes in one of his many goals for Newcastle United.

BELOW: Milburn beats the Charlton defence and Sam Bartram to score.

BARTRAM

him. And that's not usual, I can tell you.

In those days you played football out of a mixture of pride and love. Superstars hadn't been invented and, looking back, I've got to admit our wages were a little on the low side. Not that it mattered much to us. We wouldn't have swapped our experiences for all the gold in Fort Knox. For winning three Cup Finals I received less than £80, including bonuses. My weekly wage was £12 in winter and £8 in summer, and whenever we won a match there was a £2 bonus all round. 'Come on, lads,' Joe used to say. 'We've got to get the groceries.' And he was right. Most of the bonus did get spent on little extras for the wife and kids.

On long away trips, such as to London, each of us would receive one packet of Player's cigarettes on the train journey down and another on the way back. I always got a couple of extra packs because George Robledo, a non-smoker, gave me his. We really appreciated those little luxuries and I've always maintained that we were hard to beat in London because of those packets of Player's!

I suppose at this stage I ought to tell you something about myself, and how I came to fall in love with Newcastle United. Partly of course it's in the blood. Ours has been a footballing family since the days when my grandfather, Jack Milburn, used to play for

MILBURN

UFTON

CAMPBELL

Northumberland before the turn of the century. Then there were my cousins Jack Milburn (Leeds), George (Leeds and Chesterfield), Jim (Leeds) and Stan (Chesterfield and Leicester), plus their sister Cissie's two little lads who grew up to become Bobby and Jackie Charlton, World Cup winners. In case you find all this a bit confusing, I've drawn up a family tree at the front of the book for easy reference.

I was born in the upstairs flat of my grandparents' home at 14 Sixth Row, Ashington, in Northumberland. From my bedroom you could see the pityard and the shaft leading down to the coalface. It was a familiar view in the North East in the mid-twenties and one which drew most of the lads like a magnet. The money to be made down the pit—and the beer it could buy—spoilt many a promising football career. Certainly it prevented my Dad, Alec Milburn, from making the big time. He could have gone to Tottenham but preferred to stay home and drink his ale.

I was christened John Edward Thompson, after my mother's father, and that fact allied to my natural speed made it inevitable that later on in my life sportswriters would pounce on my initials, JET, to describe my style.

Right from the start I was mad about football. At school I either played left-back or outside-right and once, disastrously, centre-forward. You can't get more diverse than that, but unfortunately no one ever 'discovered' me. It wasn't until halfway through the Second World War that I got my first big break. Just before the start of the 1943-44 season, when I was 19 years old and working as a pit engineer, I spotted an advert in the local paper inviting young players to write for a trial at St James's. My pal Ray Poxton had better handwriting than I did so he wrote in for both of us.

'The toon', as Geordies call Newcastle United, gave me a game in midweek, and I was lucky enough to score two goals in one half. As a result I was chosen for the final public trial against Newcastle's first team the following Saturday. Long before the two o'clock kick-off I arrived at the ground with my boots in a brown paper parcel and sat on the steps outside eating a couple of pies for my dinner, hardly the ideal way to prepare for a big game.

Many of Newcastle's best players were away fighting the war but they still fielded the likes of my great hero Albert Stubbins, Scottish international Jimmy Gordon and one of the finest left-halves in the

JACKIE MILBURN, marked with an X, in the Hirst East Boys side which won their league title in season 1937–38.

game, Duggie Wright, was on Army leave. The game was billed as The Stripes v. The Blues and, for the first time in my life, I was allowed to wear the famous stripes. Even so, Stubbins scored twice during the first half and by half-time we were three goals down. Joe Richardson, one of the trainers, wasn't one to mince his words: 'You better buck up your ideas, son, if you want to come here,' he told me. I decided it was all or nowt in the second half.

Believe it or not, I managed to score six goals after the interval as we rattled in a total of nine against the first-teamers. At last I was on my way. The *Sunday Sun* referred to me as 'a tall youth who showed a great capacity for quick attack and opportunism' adding that, with training, I could have a bright future. The words were music to my ears.

Forty-eight hours later I was back at St James's with my Dad to see the boss, Stan Seymour. Stan was

an amazing man, and an extremely shrewd wheeler-dealer to boot. He was responsible for bringing some of the greatest post-war talent to Newcastle and, despite what anyone might say, he deserves much of the credit for our three FA Cup wins.

The moment we entered his office Stan slid his arm round my Dad's shoulder and led him towards the desk saying, 'Come on, Alec. Let's have a drink.' Out came the whisky bottle and before long Dad was pie-eyed. I was sitting in a chair immediately behind Stan when I suddenly noticed that he had his hand behind his back. In it were two five-pound notes—my signing on fee—and he fingered them like a magician fanning out a pack of cards. I'd never seen so much money in my life and I was mesmerised. I couldn't sign quickly enough.

That was on the Monday. The following Saturday, 28 August 1943, to be precise, I made my debut in

Newcastle's first team at Bradford City. Because we were leaving on the eight o'clock train from the Central Station the Club put Dad and me in an hotel in town. Dad had never stayed in such a posh place in his life and we sat up until one o'clock talking and smoking. We were in bed little more than a couple of hours before, too excited to sleep, we got up, opened the window and sat gazing out over the sombre, grey station forecourt as the dawn broke through.

I played inside-left that day but City's inside right—one Joe Harvey—scored two goals and we lost 2–1. A week later in the return at St James's I marked

RIGHT: The famous Milburn slide.

ON tour in South Africa and Newcastle players George Robledo, Alf McMichael, Charlie Crowe, Jackie Milburn, Billy Foulkes and Frank Brennan meet two of the locals.

11

TREATMENT was a bit more primitive then—Jackie with physiotherapist Alec Mutch.

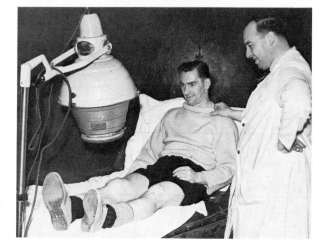

MILBURN leaves Wolves defender Shorthouse trailing. Looking on is Bobby Mitchell.

12

NEWCASTLE UNITED pictured in Montreal on their Canadian tour of 1949.

my home debut with a goal struck left-footed from 10 yards out at the Leazes End. This time we won 3–2.

During the war some clubs did little more than wait for their old players to return. United used this time differently, adopting a policy of bringing in youngsters to form part of the promotion side of 1948. As a result, players like Bobby Cowell, Ernie Taylor, Charlie Crowe, George Hair and myself all gained valuable experience.

However the war cut deeply and cruelly into the career of Albert Stubbins, a goalscorer at Newcastle and a footballer at Liverpool. He was a gentleman, the epitome of what a professional footballer should be. He scored a staggering 244 goals in 199 games for United during the war and to play alongside him as a youngster was an education in itself. He was a bit pacy was Albert and one of my abiding memories was putting spikes on with him and managing to beat him in a sprint. I idolised the man and learned from him the dignity and humility needed to help carry the burden of being a 'star', just as I'd learned from the great Raich Carter as a 13-year-old attending my first football match at Roker Park.

Billy Clark, a well-known local boxer, had taken me to the game and when Raich ran out he looked immaculate, hair slicked perfectly into shape and stockings showing precisely the right number of inches of white turn-over.

'If you ever want to be a professional footballer you must look like him,' Billy told me. A few years later Carter emphasised the point when he said to me: 'If you don't look the part you'll never be the part.'

United made a few astute buys at the end of the war including Len Shackleton from Bradford for £13,000. At this time I was a fitter at Hazelrigg Colliery and the Club got Shack a job as my labourer ... can you imagine that? It's hard to think of the highly skilled and artistic Shackleton being skivvy to anyone but these were difficult times and when it came to football we were still semi-pro.

We had a lot of fun together—I had a motor-bike even though they were banned by the Club because they were too dangerous and we used to roar round the countryside on it thoroughly enjoying ourselves.

We even rode on the bike to St James's every Tuesday and Thursday morning for training, stashing it round the back out of sight and walking into the ground. If the Club had known two such valuable assets were risking their necks at least twice a week they would have gone spare.

Shack never did anything by halves. On his debut against Newport County (a game we won 13–0) he scored six goals, a Division Two record, and put the last one in off his backside. Ever the showman, Shack always preferred to get applause for some daft trick rather than scoring a straight-forward goal.

Len never forgave Arsenal for turning him down as a kid and whenever we were playing in London he wouldn't train with us that week. He'd be off on his own practising his party pieces. He was determined to grab the headlines every time he played in London and came up with one original trick after the other, his ability was phenomenal.

Before the start of the golden era which was to bring us promotion to the First Division and three FA Cups wins at Wembley there was one final lesson still to be learned.

It came in the 1946–47 season when we reached the semi-final of the Cup and took on Charlton Athletic at Leeds. The rumblings in the camp didn't augur well. Both Joe Harvey and Len Shackleton said before the game that they would never play for Newcastle United again because they had been promised a house by the Club and hadn't got one. That was bad enough but when the manager, George Martin, dropped top scorer Charlie Wayman and put in George Stobbart at centre-forward the balloon went up.

We got turned over badly 4–0 though Peter Croker (brother of FA secretary Ted) kicked three shots off the line in the first 10 minutes before Don Welsh hit the goals trail. Suddenly we were failures and didn't like the feeling. That was the last time there was real discontent in the Club because we all learned from the Charlton debacle. The Club learned that you can't mess about the players and the players learned that you can't mess about the supporters.

The next year we were in business, promoted after playing in front of a record average attendance of 56,351 which stood until Manchester United cracked it recently. The whole place hummed. You couldn't shoe-horn all the people into St James's. There were 15,000 applications for the 1,500 season tickets and even we, the players, had to queue to get into the ground on match days.

The size of the crowd meant that it sometimes took us up to three-quarters of an hour to walk up the bank and round to the players' entrance. But what could we do? Our supporters were a marvellous warm-hearted lot. They even flooded the club with clothing coupons to help kit out the side.

That 1947–48 season carried extra significance for me because it marked my move to centre-forward after playing first at inside-left and then on the wing. It all came about because Charlie Wayman was transferred as a result of a certain incident in the dressing-room. We had a lot of top-class players in those days, and one day Charlie, who had been

getting a bit fed up, walked in to find all the pegs taken. 'Bloody hell', he said. 'I can't even get a peg in the dressing-room now. I'm off.' and off he went, to Southampton for £10,000.

George Martin decided to hand me the No 9 shirt, but I wasn't too keen because I had a complex after playing there once at school and missing so many sitters. Anyway, I went in at Bury and Lady Luck smiled on me. Bury lost their goalkeeper George Bradshaw with a broken leg in the first five minutes and Harry Catterick, later to win fame as Everton manager, went between the posts. I scored three goals against 10 men and was made. The first one was a fluke with the ball bobbling between my legs but the nice thing about goals is they all count.

By the end of the season I was United's top scorer, with 20 goals, 11 more than my nearest rival Geordie Stobbart, but by this time the team had changed significantly. Shack, Tommy Pearson and Roy Bentley as well as Wayman had all been transferred.

The first of my 13 full England caps came the following season against Ireland at Windsor Park, Belfast when I replaced Tommy Lawton at centre-forward. England were bursting with big names— Billy Wright, Frank Swift, Neil Franklin, Tom Finney, Stan Mortensen and Henry Cockburn—and they all came across in the dressing-room to have a quiet word of encouragement. All that is except the biggest name of all, Stanley Matthews. The great man never looked my way and I felt uneasy, but once we were out on the field, just before the kick-off, he shuffled across to me: 'I didn't say much in there,' he said, 'because it's out here that matters. Just get across to the far post when I have the ball and you'll be okay. Sometimes it'll hang when I cross it so give it time.'

I duly noted the advice and it worked a treat. The first time Matthews got away down the right I made for the back post, positioning myself some 10 yards out. Sure enough, the cross came high and deep. Two defenders jumped for the ball in front of me but I waited a split second before taking off. The cross hung and they were on their way down as I was on my way up which gave me that little bit extra height advantage and my header whipped into the net sweet as you like. I scored on my England debut because I listened to Stanley Matthews and we went on to win 6–2.

THE famous Milburn Clan—left to right, George Milburn (Leeds United), Jack Milburn (Leeds United), Jimmy Milburn (Leeds United), Jackie Milburn (Newcastle United), Stan Milburn (Chesterfield and Leicester), Bob and Cissie Charlton, Jackie Charlton (Leeds United) and Bobby Charlton (Manchester United).

OUR SECOND HOME

THREE times we went to Wembley. Three times we were outsiders. And three times we won the Cup. The fabulous 'fifties were ours. Each time we walked between those twin towers we knew we couldn't lose. If we'd had enough inducement I'm certain we could have done the League and Cup double, but to us only the Cup really mattered. Perhaps that sounds crazy but you have to be a Geordie, brought up black and white from the cradle, to understand what the Cup means in these parts. It's glory, glamour, drama, excitement and, above all, it's instant. United and their fans have always loved a stage upon which to perform. Wembley was our stage.

In our day there were no European cup competitions as an extra incentive so to us there was no end product in the League. The title can be won on any ground in the country on a Wednesday night or Saturday afternoon or even when you're not playing, providing the right team loses. Derby County even took the title sitting on their backsides in Majorca on holiday!

But Wembley, with a crowd of 100,000 people and millions more looking in on television, is a setting second to none. Certainly we set our caps at that and nothing else. In 1951, for example, we stopped playing League games after the semis and won only one game out of 11. What if we did chuck away a good chance of the title? We still spoilt Matthews' Wembley party. We always had to have a reason for winning. I remember the lads once reading in the Saturday papers that Derby County, who had Steele, Morris and Luty in their line-up, had gone 12 games unbeaten. From that moment they were dead . . . we just had to take their record. Right or wrong that's the

JACKIE MILBURN'S two memorable goals which beat Blackpool in the 1951 F.A. cup final at Wembley.

sort of team we were.

I scored in every round on the way to the '51 final and, in fact, should have become the first player ever to score a hat-trick in a Wembley Cup final. Before my first goal, I had the ball in the net chesting it down and sticking it between George Farm's legs but it was chalked off by the ref. Hand ball, he said, but he was wrong—I never touched it. Stan Mortensen took the hat-trick record a couple of years later when Matthews eventually got his winner's medal. I was pleased for Morty who was one of the first to inspire me when I was a kid. He was playing at Ashington in those days and I was a ball boy. He's a smashing bloke. After I scored my first goal running from the halfway line to beat Farm he came across as I returned to the centre circle, shook me by the hand, and said: 'Jackie, if we have to lose I'm glad it's to a goal like that.' Can you imagine many opponents doing that today?

I've already said that, for skill as well as for spirit, the '51 team was the best I've played with or watched during the last 30 years so I think it's worth recording the names. They were: Fairbrother, Cowell, Corbett, Harvey, Brennan, Crowe, Walker, Taylor, Milburn, Robledo (G), Mitchell.

The big boss was Stan Seymour, who was always reminding us about how he'd won the Cup in 1924 and, as all footballers will tell you, there's nothing more galling than the gaffer going on about success in his day. But he was crafty, was Stan, and he knew what would egg us on. It certainly worked!

Stan knew soccer inside out and had a knack for collecting talent. What's more, he handled the players marvellously. We might have been paupers in comparison with today's stars but we were treated like kings. Everything was first-class with Newcastle United, and everyone knew it. We had our own special carriage attached to the back of the train when we travelled away and our own chef to prepare our food. Special training at either Blackpool, Brighton or Buxton was a feature of our Cup years because Seymour believed the best way to know each other was to live together. Besides, we were paid an extra £2 a day spending money and we looked forward to that.

We were all men to Stan, not little boys. Joe Harvey believed that a couple of pints of Guinness on a Saturday morning were good for him so he was allowed to have them.. Often on a Friday night Stan would stride up to the hotel bar and buy Ernie Taylor a pint, with little Ernie hardly able to see over the top of the counter. It was all above board and in

17

moderation which is better than having players sneak round the corner for a bevvy. No fewer than nine of our team smoked and on three occasions at Wembley in a Cup final I've sat at half-time having a fag. Doing what comes naturally relaxed us and brought out the best results.

One of the lovely things about Cup finals is meeting royalty and other important people. In 1951 King George VI attended his last Cup final. He looked an ill man, brave to be there at all. In '52 we received the Cup from Winston Churchill, the greatest hero of my life whose bust has occupied pride of place in our house since 1948; and in 1955 the Queen and Prince Philip did the honours.

When we were introduced to Winston Churchill before the kick-off he smiled at me and said: 'Are you going to grab the headlines again this year?' It really impressed me that a man like that should take notice

RIGHT: The official programme for the '51 Cup final, priced one shilling.

BELOW: Going into battle against Blackpool.

AND bringing the Cup home to Tyneside afterwards.

19

HERE you are—Winston Churchill hands over the Cup to captain Joe Harvey in 1952 and The Queen does the honours in 1955 with Jimmy Scoular the skipper this time.

NO wonder he looks happy—Joe Harvey in 1952.

of a pit lad. I still consider it a compliment of the highest order.

En route to the 1952 final we had two wins which were remarkable for outstanding individual performances. In the fourth round we beat a highly talented Tottenham side 3–0 at White Hart Lane. The pitch was a mudheap that day, but Mitch was in superlative form and gave Alf Ramsey the biggest runaround of his life. A couple of rounds later we won 4–2 at Portsmouth. This game saw all 22 players giving everything they had, and was simply the best match I've ever played in. I grabbed most of the headlines with a hat-trick but, being a modest fellow, I prefer to leave the comments to others. Some of them were over the top, to say the least.

Ivan Sharpe headlined his article: JACKIE MILBURN IS THE BEST CENTRE-FORWARD IN THE WORLD and went on: 'It was Milburn who carried the Newcastle attack on his shoulders; Milburn

THE goal that beat Arsenal in '52. George Robledo's header leaves George Swindin helpless.

who equalised with an injured arm pressed to his side; Milburn who completed the hat-trick with two more individual goals—one of great subtlety and the other of spectacular thrill; and Milburn who just on time raced away again and gave George Robledo the fourth point.'

Frank Coles stated: 'It will always be remembered as Milburn's match. He had all the tricks and I have never seen a more masterly

21

CHAIRING Joe—left to right, Alf McMichael, Ronnie Simpson, Billy Foulkes, Jackie Milburn, Frank Brennan, George Robledo, Bobby Mitchell, and Bobby Cowell.

exhibition.' But just as pleasing was his assessment of Newcastle as cup fighters. He called us the finest of all modern Cup teams, better than Bolton Wanderers of the 20's and Arsenal of the 30's and added: 'They have now built the perfect football machine.'

I rate my third goal against Pompey and another I scored against Tottenham in our promotion season as my best ever. At Pompey I ran 40 yards from my own half beating tackles from Froggatt and Gunter to 25 yards out on the left side before hitting a left-foot cross shot which beat Butler. Against Tottenham at the Park we lost Dougie Graham and beat them with 10 men. It was another rocket job: Ted Ditchburn later said it was the hardest shot he'd ever faced. Memories like that certainly keep you warm in your old age!

The 1952 final against Arsenal was something of a disappointment. We won 1–0 through a George Robledo header late in the game and while we were still a tremendous Cup fighting outfit, as Frank Coles remarked, we hadn't quite the edge of the previous year. There was no Fairbrother, no Corbett, Crowe,

or Taylor. As well as this, the game was spoilt as a spectacle when Arsenal lost Wally Barnes early on because of injury, just as Manchester City were to lose Jimmy Meadows in 1955.

I always hated playing against 10 men and was a great advocate of the substitutes rule which is now accepted in soccer. In fact I'd go further and have five players stripped and on the bench. We knew we would beat both Arsenal and City anyway but when you're doubly sure because the opposition is down to 10 men it becomes harder, not easier. You get more slap-dash thinking: If I miss it doesn't matter, so-and-so will score, and the game drifts on and on.

After the final we went to South Africa on tour and received permission from the FA to take the Cup, the first time it had been allowed to leave the country. The tour lasted 10 weeks and for the first five I couldn't play. I was left at base with director Wally Hurford while the lads gallivanted all over the veldt. I had a kick from Don Roper, who moved to right-back when Barnes was injured, and I needed constant attention from the specialists. I didn't blame him for

SHAKING hands with famous people at the Cup final—Jackie with King George VI in 1951, Winston Churchill in 1952 and the Duke of Edinburgh in 1955.

23

JACKIE MILBURN heads home the fastest goal ever scored in a Wembley Cup final after 45 seconds against Manchester City in 1955.

what he'd done. After all he only wanted what I'd got the previous year, a winner's medal.

The following season I suffered the only really serious injury of my career, as a result of which I had to have a cartilage operation. Believe it or not I was playing again in less than six weeks. I wouldn't have done only director William McKeag, a man I respected, asked me to have a run out in the third team at Wallsend and promised me 'a little something' for supposedly adding a bit of glamour to the match. As it happened I got nothing, not that I'd wanted anything in the first place, and my appearance caused more than a spot of bother. Twelve thousand folk turned up to watch us at a little colliery welfare-type ground designed to hold about twelve hundred. We won 2–1 with me scoring one of the goals, but this sparked off violent protests from the opposition who would have won the League title but for that defeat.

We missed out on the Cup that year and the next but we were back at Wembley in 1955 to beat Manchester City 3–1 with three of us—Cowell, Mitchell and myself—picking up our third winner's medal.

I almost didn't make that final. The manager, Dougald Livingstone, dropped me from the team even though I'd battled throughout the season to overcome a pulled muscle in the stomach (a bad injury for a footballer) and had equalised in the dying seconds against Nottingham Forest and laid on two for Alan Monkhouse to win the second replay. When Livingstone offered his team at a directors' meeting before Wembley, it was promptly chucked out. I was reinstated, and shortly afterwards he was sacked.

Frankly, I had little respect for Livingstone. I remember him once in training putting a chalk mark on Bobby Mitchell's boot showing him how to sidefoot a ball properly. Magical Mitch, of all people, probably the best placer of a ball we had! I was never in Livingstone's clique so perhaps I shouldn't have been surprised by anything he did.

Just before the match Stan Seymour, who had led the 'Newcastle don't play in Cup finals without Milburn' campaign, said to me: 'Go out and show them, Jackie.' I did just that. Seconds into the game I won a corner on the right and Len White went over to take it. City's captain Roy Paul was standing next to me as White placed the ball when he suddenly yelled: 'Bloody hell, I should be marking Keeble' and darted off to find big Vic, noted for his prowess in the air.

White fired the ball in my direction and there I was standing all alone like Grey's Monument. I headed the ball past Bert Trautmann and that was it: the fastest ever Wembley goal.

My heading was always something of a joke among the lads but in reality I could head as well as the next fella as long as I was on my own. Throughout my playing career I suffered from fibrositis and was terrified of jumping with anyone in case my neck 'stuck'. If it did I was unable to do anything except lie in bed and my wife literally had to clean my teeth.

Funnily enough my complaint was completely cured ten years ago when I was visiting the beautiful little seaside town of Seahouses. I remember standing watching a man exercising some horses when he suddenly came over to me, introduced himself as Brigadier General Bolton and said: 'You're Milburn, aren't you?' After we had talked for a time the conversation turned to my fibrositis, of which the Brigadier said he could cure me. He told me to take Kruschen salts in hot water or tea every morning for at least five weeks and, after years of agony I was willing to try anything. Somewhat to my surprise, it worked and from that time on I've had no more trouble.

The Club had spent a fortune on trying to help me and I hate to think how many goals I might have headed had I been fully fit. I reckon fibrositis cost me more than 50 goals over my career as a whole, but in spite of that little handicap I still hold the Newcastle United goal-scoring record with 178 League goals between 1946 and 1957. And anyway, for a centre-forward whose heading was supposed to be a joke I didn't do too badly. I scored at Wembley in a Cup Final, scored on my debut for England, and got two headers in my only England hat-trick against Wales and my bogey-man Tommy Jones of Everton.

But I was talking about Wembley 1955. Our skipper Jimmy Scoular kept spraying great crossfield balls to Bobby Mitchell and between them they tore City apart. Mitch put us back in front after City had equalised, and George Hannah wrapped it all up with a 12-yarder after another Scoular-Mitchell combination. I played most of the match carrying an injury but it didn't matter. I'd made my point and put us on our way. I was satisfied and, I hope, I had justified Seymour's faith in me.

After the match I took the Cup home to Ellington Terrace in Ashington and stood it in a corner of the room while we all rabbited on about our win. We

were much too excited to notice that my daughter Betty, a toddler at the time, promptly picked up the Cup and dragged it off outside. The first we knew was when we heard shouts from the back lane. 'Daddy, Daddy!', she was calling. 'Look what I'm doing!' When I got out there I couldn't believe my eyes. That lovely silver pot, everyone's pride and joy, was caked in dirt and full to the brim of the most disgusting mixture you've ever seen.

'I'm making mud pies,' explained Betty tri-

NEWCASTLE UNITED players ride through the streets of the city after winning the Cup for the third time in five years.

umphantly, arms up to the elbows in liquid mud and squelching the stuff through her fingers. We all stood horrified, with visions of the Football Association's most prized possession defaced beyond redemption. I still feel a sense of relief every time I see the Cup raised to the Wembley rafters glinting in its pefection. It's amazing what a bit of elbow grease will do.

Apart from Betty we have two other children, Linda and Jackie and I like to think I got them a Cup winner's medal each. As for my wife Laura . . . well, I kid her that she got me, didn't she? On a sadder note, two members of that 1955 team have since had their gongs pinched, and both, irony of ironies, on Cup Final days. Joe Harvey was burgled in 1975 and Mitch the following year. Gold was high on the market then and it's almost certain that they were melted down. If the thieves had realised the sweat and tears which went into gaining those medals I'm certain they would have found something else to nick. To us they are irreplaceable.

DONE UP TO THE NINES

HUGHIE GALLACHER, the man who started it all.

THERE'S always been something romantic about a centre-forward. The position invariably conjures up that comic-strip hero, Roy of the Rovers swooping down on goal, scoring with blistering shots, and being carried shoulder high in triumph from the pitch. Well, link centre-forwards with Newcastle United and you have true romance. United and centre-forwards go hand in hand and throughout the Club's illustrious history there have always been good ones. The fans adore them, turn them into instant heroes, worship them in a way no player in any other position can hope to be worshipped.

Some fifty or so yards from St James's Park stands a supporter's club which even boasts a 'No. 9' bar decorated with framed photographs of black-and-white heroes and shirts worn by the greats. It's only to be expected in a place like Newcastle.

It all started with the incomparable Hughie Gallacher, but since then centre-forwards have come in all shapes and sizes. Remember Albert Stubbins, Charlie Wayman, Vic Keeble, Len White, Wyn Davies, Malcolm Macdonald, Peter Withe? And that's just for starters. There were many, many more, but one thing is certain: we all owe our heritage to wee Hughie. He began it all, the hero worship and the affinity with the No 9. Sadly, not many readers will have seen Hughie play because he did his stuff a long time ago but legends live on, and on Tyneside he is part of folklore.

Gallacher, who was in the famous Scotland Blue Devils, still holds two records at Newcastle—he scored the most League goals in a season, 36, when United last won the First Division championship in 1927 and the Club's attendance record of 68,586 was set when Hughie came 'back home' with Chelsea in September, 1930.

Even as a small child I remember a song we used to sing in the school playground. It went like this: 'Do you ken Hughie Gallacher the wee Scots lad, the best centre-forward Newcastle ever had'. I'm not going to argue with that.

Years later I was fortunate enough to wear Hughie's shirt and virtually every Saturday he'd be waiting for me outside the main entrance, always at the same time in the same place, ten yards from the door. 'Hi, Jackie, you're doing fine,' he'd say, 'but I've got a little tip for you . . .' Then he would mention something he had spotted in my play the previous game.

'You're standing with your back to the centre-half and your team-mates don't know how to play the ball up to you. Why don't you half turn to give them a clue which side you want it and then run. They'll never catch you.'

Throughout my playing days I always listened intently to any advice the big names had to give. To me their words were worth a million from any coach. I only once played with the great Hughie and that was in a charity match when he was 52 years of age. He took a cross from the wing, jammed it against the goal post with his head, and dropped it over the line—who

ALBERT STUBBINS, an early inspiration to Jackie Milburn.

VIC KEEBLE, devastating in the air.

else could do a thing like that? I literally wept the day I learned he had walked onto the railway crossing just outside Newcastle and put his neck across the line to finish it all. How a man so loved and so idolised could feel so alone I'll never know.

Over the years I shared the attack with a number of centre-forwards from Stubbins and Wayman through to Keeble and White. Albert Stubbins was never

ALL centre-forwards together—
Charlie Wayman, Len White,
Ron McGarry, Peter Withe, Al-
bert Stubbins, Billy Cairns and
Jackie Milburn.

BRIAN CLOUGH, an England No. 9 himself for 'the other lot' as well as manager of twice European Cup winners Nottingham Forest, admires Hughie Gallacher's plaque in the No. 9 bar of the Newcastle Supporters' Association.

LEN WHITE as Newcastle fans remember him.

a man to brag—except once. He was sitting next to me in the dressing-room before a game against Bolton when he leaned across and said quietly: 'I'll score three today, Jackie.' He did, too, all in the first half and each one brilliant in its own way. His goalscoring years, as I've already said, came while he was wearing the black-and-white shirt rather than the red of Liverpool, and that followed a natural pattern amongst strikers.

Up to the age of 22 or 23 you have no fear, just an instinct for scoring goals. Then the Press start heaping praise on you and with all the attention you begin to think you can play. You start to pick your spot instead of lashing the ball instinctively and, more often than not, it will strike a post rather than go in. In other words you lose what the public wants. It happens to most of us at some time and it happened to Albert Stubbins after he left United. Some get it back, others are never quite the same hungry goal machine. The best example is Bobby Charlton, who scored so many

WYN DAVIES climbs high above Chelsea's David Webb.

stunning goals early in his career but never quite retained his output once he became a 'famous footballer'.

Charlie Wayman suffered no such problems. He realised what he was best at and stuck to it. He never lost the urge and even in a five-a-side match he would punch the sky in delight after a goal a kid could have scored. He was Johnny-on-the-spot, invaluable to wingers. With Wayman, Malcolm Macdonald or George Robledo, if they didn't score they weren't worth watching but there was always the feeling that at any moment they might make your hair stand on end and, when you boil it all down, that's what football is all about.

Keeble was nicknamed 'the Camel' for two reasons. He hunched his shoulders which made him look as though he had a hump on his back and he couldn't kick a ball to save his soul. But, my oh my, was he useful in the air. When Vic got the ball he treated it like a hot potato. He couldn't get rid of it fast enough and he didn't care where to. Most players prefer to head either to the right or the left but Keeble could do it either way with equal effect. He scored so many goals with his nut that I swear he had studs in his forehead.

Len White was, for me, the best Newcastle United player never to be capped for England. He had pace, good close control and was an effortless finisher but he was short and that doesn't help. Had he been two inches taller my guess is he'd have become England's centre-forward. He nearly made it when he scored a hat-trick for the Football League at Goodison, but somehow the selectors still hesitated. I was playing for Linfield at the time and I travelled over specially to watch him. There was a long gap between my last cap against Denmark in 1956 and the next Newcastle player to gain an England cap, Malcolm Macdonald in 1972, and White should have bridged that gap. If I had to criticise him it would be to say he had a tendency to withdraw into his shell if things didn't go right in the first 10 minutes but normally he would take on the world and win.

One player who will always have a place in the hearts of Tynesiders is Ron McGarry. He may not have had the class of some of the people I've mentioned, but he was interesting all the same. He was the forerunner of Malcolm Macdonald, the first bragger who talked as hard as he could shoot. You could say that McGarry was Cassius Clay, as SuperMac was Muhammad Ali.

MALCOLM MACDONALD in typical pose with his partner Terry Hibbitt offering congratulations.

McGarry used to tell me: 'Those lot are thoroughbreds, I'm an amateur but if I can't play I may as well frighten the opposition to death by talking.' He was a real character, and marvellous in the dressing-room where he quickly dispelled any gloom hanging around. Ron actually had visiting cards printed which read: 'Ron McGarry, have goals—will travel' and he used to dish them out at the players' entrance of St James's Park.

His claim to fame was that he was United's top scorer when they won the Second Division champion-ship in 1965. In 31 appearances he scored 16 goals which proved he wasn't the lame duck some people thought. Joe Harvey had bought him from Bolton to do precisely that job after giving him his first chance at Workington when, I might add, he could easily have become a Rugby League player with Whitehaven rather than a soccer player.

Between the two talkers, McGarry and Macdonald, we had a bloke called Wyn Davies who was instrumental in helping United win the Fairs Cup in 1969. This was Newcastle's first experience in Europe

IT'S in the net and Leeds United's Paul Reaney and David Harvey are beaten by SuperMac. John Tudor turns away in delight.

and they sailed through to lift the Fairs Cup (now rechristened the UEFA Cup) because the Continentals couldn't master Wyn the Leap in the air. United used to flood high balls into the box and Wyn did the rest.

Joe Harvey fancied both Francis Lee and Davies at Bolton and tried to sign them both but Franny was in business and didn't want to move too far away. Wyn was extremely difficult to sign for a different reason. He was a suspicious, reticent man by nature, made even more so by the fact that early in his career a club had promised him some cash which never materia-

lised. When Newcastle approached him he was understandably cautious. Club director Wilf Taylor also happened to be vice-president of the League at the time so there was no question of a back-hander and eventually it all depended on Wyn being allowed to consult his mother. With a slightly embarrassed Harvey and Mr Taylor standing by, Wyn telephoned his mother, who was waiting in a coin box at the end of the street in Caernarvon where she lived, and then proceeded to talk to her in Welsh so nobody could understand what he said.

Wyn was said to be so tight that he would even argue about the price of a newspaper. Certainly he was a loner and, like most others, I never got close to him. He was the only man ever to wear the famous No 9 black-and-white shirt who kept himself to himself. The adulation and the glamour which goes with the job opens up even the shyest of men but getting a reaction out of Wyn was like prising open a steel coffin.

Despite all this he had a warm relationship with the St James's crowd. The battle cry of the day was 'You ain't seen nothing like the Mighty Wyn' and it would come cascading from the terraces each time United demolished another Continental team.

Davies's game was all about bravery and heading ability. Unlike Keeble he never got a sackful of goals himself—indeed two years after winning the Fairs Cup he scored only two First Division goals in the whole of the season. But his worth to others, especially Pop Robson, was immeasurable.

For sheer excitement Malcolm Macdonald was the boyo. He arrived at the park in a Rolls-Royce and he did everything in style until the day he left. He had a one-track mind—goals, goals and more goals. Nothing else, outside of his family, mattered. I've never known any player, and I include the great Jimmy Greaves, who retained his appetite for goals the way Macdonald did. Looking back, I only wish I'd had some of his single-mindedness.

Once he smelt the goal his eyes narrowed into slits and he looked like a hunter stalking his prey. He was convinced he would score every time and that was his secret. If he hit the corner flag with a shot it did nothing to undermine his confidence. Lots of players look for a hole to hide in after such a miss and if it happens again they want to die. Not him.

There are two kinds of bravery on the football pitch. There's the type where a player clatters someone so hard it rattles their teeth and there's the

BIG time charlie—Malcolm Macdonald with cigar and champagne, an image he deliberately created and which the fans adored.

sort where a player has the courage to pit his skill against others, to beat two or three men in a long run with the ball. I like to think I had the latter kind of bravery. Macdonald certainly did. He was often accused of playing for himself, which was true up to a point. But then all key players do that and the team still benefits.

He had explosive pace and power, a murderous left foot and was aggressive in the air. His speed was critical to his game but what few people realised was that he had asthma trouble which prevented him from making two 30 or 40 yard sprints without taking a breather in between. He admitted the problem to me during one of our many long conversations but never played on it publicly.

Mac got off to a flyer with the fans by scoring a hat-trick against mighty Liverpool on his home debut—a feat I rate as possibly even greater than Shack's six-goal debut against Newport County. Joe Harvey missed Macdonald's three because he was away scouting—or was he frightened that, having spent a record £180,000, it might turn out that the brash youngster with the horseshoe legs was all wind and water? I've often kidded Joe about it but in reality he

deserves enormous credit for signing a player who hadn't kicked a ball in the First Division and turned out to be a gem.

Before long even SuperMac's transfer fee seemed quite reasonable. Peter Withe set a new mark when he arrived fresh from leading Nottingham Forest to the First Division championship in exchange for a £250,000 cheque. After a short spell with United he was sold to Aston Villa for half a million pounds in the summer of 1980.

Peter was all left foot (his right was strictly for standing on) but his strength was in the air and that, coupled with an insatiable appetite for work, made him a formidable leader of a line, if not a natural goalscorer. If Withe didn't function neither did the team a fact which cost United promotion two seasons ago, but equally he was incapable of making things happen himself. He relied too much on other players, whatever their calibre. In short he wasn't a match winner, but even so at Villa he proved Brian Clough wrong when he boasted that any player sold by Forest was never a success afterwards. And Withe certainly had his good side. He was one of the friendliest 'foreigners' ever to come to the North East, and a most likeable lad.

39

PETER WITHE shows his elation at scoring.

FAIRS
CUP
GLORY

THE old Fairs Cup will never be forgotten on Tyneside. For three seasons starting in 1968 Newcastle United took Europe by storm and filled St James's Park to capacity as a succession of glamorous Continental sides came over to challenge their authority. It was romantic and exciting, an adventure into the unknown with a promise of a pot of gold at the end of it all. United reached that gold, too, at their very first attempt, when they won the

European Fairs Cup in 1969—the first and only time United's name has been written into the pages of Europe's soccer annals.

United qualified for the Fairs Cup under the one-city-one-club rule at a time when they were lying only 10th in the First Division. But it didn't seem to matter. They went on to score glorious victories over the Dutch wizards Feyenoord, Sporting Lisbon, Real Zaragoza, Vittoria Setubal, Glasgow Rangers and

SETUBAL beaten in a snowstorm at St. James's with Wyn Davies again in the thick of it.

POP ROBSON opens up the Setubal defence to try a left foot shot.

finally the crack Hungarian side Ujpest Dozsa. But amid all the glamour and success came tragedy for at least one player. Football's like that: you never quite know when Fate is going to take a hand. The player I'm referring to is Geoff Allen, a ruddy-faced 21-year-old who played as though in love with the left touchline, rarely straying from its side. He achieved his finest hour at the expense of Feyenoord when it all began on a Wednesday night in September 1968. His was the old fashioned artistry, caressing the ball and weaving magical spells to probe, then expose, and finally humiliate the Dutch. Allen set up United's first-ever European goal when he took a ball from Pop Robson down his own personal avenue and drove a low cross into an acre of space from which Jimmy Scott gleefully side-footed it past international goalkeeper Pieters Graafland. Seven minutes had gone and all of us in the 46,000 crowd could see what was to come. Further goals by Robson, Gibb and Davies made it a sensational 4–0 start for the Tom Thumbs of European soccer.

For Feyenoord, aristocrats, former European Cup semi-finalists, pride of their homeland, the impossible had happened. The condemned man had shot the firing squad.

In case United thought it was all easy pickings in the rich playground of the Continent the return leg quickly redressed the balance. It was far too late for Feyenoord, of course, but they played for their dignity and United took a pounding. Neither Allen nor any other forward was to see the ball and it was left to big John McNamee, the frailer Ollie Burton, and the acrobatic Iam McFaul to bear the brunt of a 2–0 defeat.

The match in Rotterdam was to mark the end of Allen's fleeting European action. Less than three

JUST about the greatest goal of the Fairs Cup Campaign—Pop Robson is off the floor as he vollies the ball past the Sporting Lisbon defence.

weeks later, playing against Nottingham Forest on County's ground, a crunching tackle by Peter Hindley laid him out in the first quarter of an hour. Geoff's knee was shattered and he only made one more senior appearance, against Sheffield Wednesday later in the same season when he lasted all of three minutes before crumbling under his own weight. Out of despair comes good, occasionally, and Allen is still at St James's as coach to the Central League team.

By way of a contrast, Bob Moncur, who scored a most unlikely hat-trick during the two-legged final, was missing through injury when the championship began. He managed to get himself stretchered off in a pre-season friendly at Hibernian and needed a cartilage operation before he was fit to play. Luckily, he recovered in time for the second hurdle against Sporting Lisbon and never looked back. What he must have been thinking as he lifted the tulip-shaped trophy high into the night air of Budapest I don't know.

This was the period which marked the emergence

LEFT: The souvenir programme for the semi-final with Rangers at St. James's.

JACKIE SINCLAIR scores the goal which beat Glasgow Rangers in the semi-final and sparked off a riot among the Scottish fans.

THE Fairs Cup Final first leg against Ujpest Dozsa at St. James's. Note the fans standing on the rooftops to get a bird's-eye view of the game.

WYN DAVIES puts Ujpest under pressure.

of two local kids, Alan Foggon and Keith Dyson, both 18. In the match which ended Geoff Allen's career Dyson was playing only his third senior game and Foggon was the sub who replaced the stricken winger. Both scored in a shock 4–2 win over Forest and four days later both did it again to help United to another mind-boggling away victory, 4–1 at Ipswich.

Foggon was a great kid, with a keen awareness of his stylistic imperfections. He was the kind of player who'd run 50 yards, beating three men, and then fall over the ball. But, despite being roly poly, he was lethal on the run and had a cannonball shot like Malcolm Macdonald's. The only trouble was he managed only two out of ten shots on the target while a top striker aims at six out of ten.

Dyson wasn't blessed with pace, which is a tremendous handicap, but he had other things. He played with his backside, using it like the rudder of a ship to manoeuvre himself into position while holding off the opposition. He could keep a ball played up to him all day, had good close control, and knew how to

pin-point his centres. I had a soft spot for both of them.

Foggon wore Allen's No 11 shirt against Sporting in Lisbon with Dyson getting on as sub and Tot Winstanley making his only European appearance for the injured McNamee. The match was played in a thunderstorm with jagged streaks of lightning flashing across the black sky. Coach Dave Smith sat on the open bench with his head swathed in a huge white towel like some heavyweight boxer waiting for the opening bell. The rain lashed down until it lapped round his ankles and, with United leading through a Jim Scott goal, the excitable Smith looked like being washed away on a tide of emotion until Sporting equalised thirty seconds from time.

Sporting's goal was a bit of a fluke. It came from a bloke called Morais who had won the European Cupwinner's Cup for Sporting four years previously. His speculative 30-yard shot was tipped onto the bar by McFaul only for it to rebound, strike Willie on the arm, and drop into the net. But 1–1 was good enough, thank you very much, and three weeks later almost 54,000 spectators saw United go through to the next round with a single goal from Pop Robson, one of the best executed efforts of the whole Fairs Cup trail. Dyson was fouled just outside the area, after which Robson ran over the ball, then away to the left distracting the Sporting defenders. Meanwhile Gibb clipped the free kick to Davies who was lurking just inside the right-hand corner of the penalty box. Davies headed strongly across the face of the goal into the path of Robson who had run round the back of the Sporting wall. The ball must have reached Pop above waist height but he didn't break stride as he jumped, both feet off the ground, to volley a truly memorable goal. The combination of the Davies knock down and the Robson finish was what ultimately fashioned United's Fairs success. Together, those two were deadly.

Big Wyn will always be remembered as the lynchpin of the side in Europe and rightly so because he achieved a darned sight more success on the Continent than at home. To our European cousins the name of the game is football, with the emphasis on foot. A big man who climbs well in the air is not only a peculiar sight to them but almost beyond control.

To my mind though Robson was the best all-round player. He had the class *and* the skill, and was at his most dangerous as a finisher coming from behind the ball, as he did against Sporting, rather than snapping up chances closer in.

The next hurdle turned out to be Bechers Brook, United clearing it safely only after clipping the top. Spain's Real Zaragoza produced the sternest challenge of the competition and forced the Magpies to edge through on the away goals rule for the one and only time. After 180 minutes the score was 4–4, consisting of a 2–3 defeat away and a 2–1 win at home.

On the away leg, on New Year's Day, 1969, United celebrated Hogmanay in the cathedral city of Zaragoza by scoring two goals which subsequently provided a passport to further glories. The old firm of Davies and Robson, did it again with a goal apiece. Davies' was a header, would you believe, and Pop's came from a low, hard Gibb cross.

Davies, a tall, lean, proud figure breathing the fire of a Welsh dragon, teased and tormented Zaragosa's lumbering giant of a centre-half Santamaria, an international with a considerable number of caps. But the Spaniards had their own attacking men of genius.

In fact, like most Continental sides United met along the way they were vulnerable in defence but highly inventive up front.

Zaragoza's winning goal in the first leg was brilliantly executed and owed much to the pace and accuracy of Argentinian winger Martin, not to mention Planas's off-the-ball running. But the two players I'll always remember were a centre-forward called Bustillo, who had just completed his national service and was only on his way to Barcelona for a bagful of pesetas, and his sidekick Marcelino, sole survivor of a forward line dubbed the 'the Magnificent Five' when Real Zaragoza lifted the Fairs Cup and Spanish Cup in 1964.

Back home for the return, the 56,200 crowd were still settling in their seats when Robson stunned everyone with a rocket goal. Taking a short Burton pass on the right wing he began to cut inside. As two defenders converged on him Pop suddenly spurted through the closing gap to unleash a vicious shot from fully 30 yards. The ball flew high into the net to the left of goalkeeper Nieves, to the astonishment of a watching Bertie Mee (later to pilot Arsenal to the League and Cup double). So lost in admiration was Bertie that he declared: 'Only Yashin or Frank Swift would have got anywhere near that shot.'

Gibb added another good goal when he headed home a Robson corner after 28 minutes, and when Nieves was injured diving at Foggon's feet it seemed like one-way traffic.

We reckoned, however, without sub-keeper Alarcia, obviously anxious to make a name for himself. He whizzed round like a Catherine wheel on Guy Fawkes' Night throwing himself all over the place to deny Newcastle a third goal. After 42 minutes Zaragoza knocked in the first Fairs Cup goal to be scored against United at St James's and the tension became almost unbearable.

The score was now 4–4 on aggregate. One more Zaragoza strike and United were out. Newcastle knew it, the Spaniards knew it, and we in the crowd knew it. You could have cut the atmosphere with a knife but at long last the ordeal was over and the home side deservedly took the final whistle in charge.

This meant United were through to the quarter-final, and drawn to play Vittoria Setubal of Portugal. Frankly, the Portuguese were beaten before they started. Even though it was March when they came to the Park the pitch was covered in snow and a blizzard was raging. Poor souls! Half of them hadn't even seen

JIM SCOTT scores Newcastle's third goal to give them a 3–0 lead on the first leg of the final.

snow before. Those lovely looking white flakes hadn't fallen on their Portuguese fishing village for 25 years and while the players were fascinated by it all before the match once out there on the pitch they very nearly froze to death. What a sight! Their so-called dusky destroyer, Jacinto Joao, played with socks pulled over his hands and stood, a pathetic forlorn figure, literally shivering out on the left wing before being substituted, obviously as an act of human kindness.

Setubal were frozen out of the competition 5–1 with goals from Robson (2), Davies, Foggon and Gibb but the weather couldn't dampen down the fervour on Tyneside. The Fairs Cup was beginning to dominate the sporting life of the city as witnessed in the gate of 57,662 snowmen.

Out there United were subjected to a lot of intimidation and several players were unsettled and distracted by the sight of fans parading round the perimeter of the ground dressed as clowns. But they survived on the strength of the first leg, and a Davies header from corner brought breathing space in a 3–1 second leg defeat.

Six weeks later came the first of the semi-finals and a clash with the only other surviving British club, Glasgow Rangers. A record Fairs Cup crowd of 75,580 (including 12,000 from Newcastle) gathered at Ibrox to witness a 0–0 draw highlighted by a telling penalty save from Iam McFaul. Andy Penman drove the spot kick hard to McFaul's right but the keeper dived to turn it round the post.

Big John McNamee, a one-time Celtic player, had caused ructions in Glasgow by saying that he could curb Rangers' Colin Stein on one leg—a typical piece of bravado from the big man. It might have rebounded on him and United but it didn't. Mac did indeed put Stein in his back pocket.

The following week Rangers crossed Hadrian's Wall with the Tartan hordes in their wake, bent on revenge. The reputation of the Scottish supporters when travelling is somewhat tarnished and, stoked up by large quantities of ale, we might have anticipated that they would take defeat badly. That they did.

After 52 minutes the dam was breached. A beautiful ball inside the full-back by Gibb saw Scott run like a deer to smash a cross shot into the far corner of the net. Twenty-five minutes later Sinclair read a Davies flick on to nip in and blast a close-range shot high past Neef. That one kick took the tie beyond the reach of Rangers forever and, faced with the inevitable, the drunken fans went berserk. A hail of

UNITED have won the Fairs Cup in Budapest and Ben Arentoft and Ollie Burton shake hands with the Ujpest players.

UNITED do a lap of honour in Budapest.

LORD WESTWOOD and coach Dave Smith drink from the Fairs Cup. In the foreground is Ben Arentoft.

beer bottles rained onto the pitch from the Gallow-gate end, followed by numerous enraged Scotsmen. The terrified players had no choice but to run for the safety of the tunnel as police with dogs fought to stem the tide.

For 17 minutes St James's resembled Bannockburn, but eventually, with the police standing shoulder to shoulder behind McFaul's goal, and a mountain of beer bottles piled against the left-hand post, the last ten minutes were played out. Yes, it was frightening, even from the safety of the Press box perched on top of the old stand but, thankfully, United's supporters remained where they belonged on the terraces and were later exonerated of all blame by an inquiry.

Eight days later came the first leg of the final, when another 60,000 paid record receipts of £42,000 to witness a historic moment. How my heart beat . . . it was like the old days again with St James's jam-packed and fans scrambling along the rooftops of houses lining the popular side of the ground to catch a glimpse of the action.

Hungary's Ujpest Dozsa provided the opposition—and what opposition. Their pedigree was impeccable. They had beaten Leeds United home and away in the semi-final to be hailed by Don Revie as 'the greatest team in Europe' and just 24 hours before they flew to England no fewer than seven of them had helped Hungary beat Czechoslovakia 2–0 in a World Cup qualifying game. They included legendary stars Ferenc Bene and skipper Janos Gorocs, once named by Bobby Charlton as one of the

51

SKIPPER Bob Moncur, who scored a hat-trick over the two-legged final, with the Fairs Cup.

finest inside-forwards he had every played against, and a tall striker called Antal Dunai who had run Eusebio close for the Golden Boot award as Europe's top marksman.

Yet United were to destroy them, at home and behind the Iron Curtain. Amazing! The men who achieved this astonishing feat were: McFaul; Craig, Clark; Gibb, Burton, Moncur; Scott, Robson, Davies, Arentoft, Sinclair. The score was still deadlocked at 0–0 after 63 minutes but during the next half-hour Ujpest were taken to the cleaners. They hadn't conceded three goals in the last two years and probably didn't know what hit them when the black-and-white tidal wave battered them into submission. A free-kick just outside the box gave United the chance to field their usual but highly successful ploy. Gibb lofted the ball towards Davies who, ten yards out, stepped back to take it on the chest. As the ball dropped, he smashed it against Szentmihalyi. Moncur, usually the penalty area defender rather than attacker, swooped to gobble up the chance left-footed. Newcastle were now 1–0 up.

With Foggon on for Sinclair, skipper Moncur left

his rearguard beat again ten minutes later to play a one-two with the Dane, Benny Arentoft and whip a daisy-cutter inside the far post. 2–0. Seven minutes from the end Arentoft again acted as a wall for Scott who lifted the return over the keeper's head as he came out. 3–0.

Heroes all, but there were special performances from two-goal Moncur, until now a marker rather than marksman, from the battle-scarred Davies and from Burton who played Bene so authoritatively. How Davies earned his corn in Europe! He'd had a spell in hospital after Feyenoord, broken his nose against Rangers and fractured his cheekbone near the end against Ujpest. Yet he never flinched from physical contact.

I actually missed the final emotion-laden 90 minutes in Budapest but listened to every minute of it on the radio, something I never usually do. I'm not a man to bother with match commentaries preferring the real thing or nothing at all but on this occasion I had to have some tenuous link with 'my Club'. I've re-lived the last hour and a half of United's Fairs Cup journey through my radio and through the co-writer of this book, John Gibson, who is as big a black-and-white fanatic as I am and who travelled with Newcastle's official party to the Hungarian capital.

An unchanged United took a first-half pounding from the Magyars who knew their only chance was an early breakthrough. On the half hour it came. Bene, on the right appeared to have no angle to shoot at as he suddenly pivoted but the ball flew as straight as an arrow into the far corner of the net and the pressure was on. Ujpest, showing the form which had reduced Leeds to mere mortals, attacked relentlessly. Only McFaul's slight frame stood in the way of Bankuti's left foot and the midfield magic of Gorocs. McFaul made a back-breaking fingertip save from an Ede Dunai 25-yarder and somehow clawed out a vicious downward header from Antal Dunai destined for the bottom corner. But then came another first-half goal which made it 2–0 and threw the whole tie back into the melting pot. It came at a killer time, too, just a couple of minutes before the interval when Gorocs took a crossfield pass in his stride to beat United's keeper at the near post.

Heavy hearts and tired legs took United to the dressing-room and the waiting Joe Harvey, 50 that day and in danger of losing his most deeply desired birthday present. David Craig recalled later that they left the field expecting Harvey to rip them apart in his

JOE HARVEY jubilantly holds up the Fairs Cup in the directors' box at St. James's Park.

anger. Instead Joe was calm and re-assuring.

'Remember you're still leading 3–2 and only 45 minutes away from lifting the Cup,' he told them. 'Grab a quick goal and Ujpest will fold, I promise you.'

Away from the clamour and the howling fans United dredged up the last of their confidence to rejoin the battle in a new mood. Unsuspecting, Ujpest moved in to sink the harpoon even deeper . . . and got caught a vicious blow. Moncur was loitering as Szentmihalyi punched out a left wing corner and when Sinclair clipped the ball back in there was the darkly dangerous skipper to complete his two-legged hat-trick with a venomous left-foot shot. The score was now 1–2, or much more significantly, 4–2 on aggregate and Ujpest, suddenly ran out of steam, as Harvey had forecast. Now it was United's turn to look good. Arentoft, a runner and a worker, levelled the game six minutes later when he pounced on a blocked shot from Scott to drive inside the left-hand post from 15 yards.

Nothing could stop United now. The team was playing superbly and the winning goal was positively breathtaking. Foggon had replaced Scott, who had cramp, and in the 76th minute he set off alone on one of those electrifying runs of his from just a couple of yards inside the Ujpest half. He nodded down a long pass to get into his stride and swept two bedraggled defenders out of his path as he hot-footed it for goal. Foggon never faltered. Once in position he struck the ball with such tremendous force that the poor keeper could only fling up a despairing hand to divert the ball onto the bar, but before he had time to move another muscle the onrushing Foggon had hurtled a shot into the net.

ABOVE: Anderlecht players bundle Wyn Davies (No. 9) into the back of the net after the Welshman had felled their keeper.

BELOW: Referee Joseph Minnoy orders off Inter Milan goalkeeper Lido Vieri at St. James's. United beat the famous Italian club 2–0.

Ujpest had been given a two-goal start on their own patch but United destroyed them. A 6–2 scoreline over the two games was a mammoth margin against such esteemed opposition. There could be no argument about United's right to call themselves the Fairs champions of Europe.

United competed for the Fairs Cup for another two seasons and can justifiably boast that they have never been eliminated from the competition by a club scoring more goals than them over the two legs. In 1969–70, after the Ujpest triumph, they were to defeat Dundee United, Oporto of Portugal and Southampton before going out in the quarter-finals to the Belgian club, Anderlecht on the away goals rule.

And in 1970–71 Harvey's men beat the might of Inter Milan before being eliminated by much inferior opposition, Pesci Dozsa, on penalty kicks in Hungary after the two clubs had tied on aggregate.

INTERNATIONAL MATCH

England v. Switzerland

on

THURSDAY, 2nd DECEMBER, 1948

DINNER

held at

THE DORCHESTER
Park Lane, W.1

Patron:
HIS MAJESTY THE KING
President:
THE RT. HON. THE EARL OF ATHLONE, K.G.
Secretary: *Chairman of the Council*:
SIR STANLEY ROUS, C.B.E., J.P.   A. BROOK HIRST, O.B.E.

ENGLAND

v.

ARGENTINA

To be played at
WEMBLEY STADIUM
on WEDNESDAY
9th MAY, 1951
kick-off 15.00 hours

PATRON :
HIS MAJESTY THE KING.
PRESIDENT :
THE RT. HON. THE EARL OF ATHLONE, K.G.
Secretary :   Chairman of Council :
Sir Stanley Rous, C.B.E.   A. Brook Hirst, O.B.E.

COUPE JULES RIMET 1950
(WORLD CUP)

BRAZIL
June 24th to July 16th
1950

PATRON :
HIS MAJESTY THE KING.
PRESIDENT :
THE RT. HON. THE EARL OF ATHLONE, K.G.
Secretary :   Chairman of Council :
S. F. ROUS, C.B.E.   A. BROOK HIRST, O.B.E.

INTERNATIONAL MATCH
IRELAND
v.
ENGLAND

To be played at
WINDSOR PARK
BELFAST
on
Saturday, 9th October, 1948

KICK-OFF 3.0 p.m.

SOME of Milburn's England honours.

WEMBLEY WILLIES

Part One

I CAN'T help feeling sad that United haven't won a Cup final since way back in 1955, however nice it may be to be associated with that winning side. Looking back, who would have thought as we trudged happily off the field that out Club would be in for such a long wait? We were the Cup fighters, don't forget, renowned throughout the land. We had just won the pot for the third time in five years and the Club boasted a hatful of records. Together with West Bromwich Albion, the black-and-whites had made more Cup final appearances than any other club—ten in all—and the trophy had been won on six occasions which was only bettered by Aston Villa's seven. Equally

significant, we were unbeaten at Wembley.

Tradition dies hard, and whenever January came round everyone started taking notice of United. That attention was justified in 1974 when Newcastle, under the management of that old warhorse Joe Harvey, knocked out all the opposition to reach the final at Wembley. Even though my position was now in the Press box instead of out on the field, I still felt a part of it all, and like Joe and the whole of Tyneside, I was delighted to be back in business once more.

In some ways, getting to Wembley is more exciting than actually playing in the Final, especially when, like Newcastle United that year, you decide to travel

ONE of SuperMac's super two goals which destroyed Burnley in the semi-final and shot United to Wembley.

HAPPY United players, some in stocking feet, return to the pitch at Hillsborough to salute the fans after winning the semi-final. Left to right, Terry Hibbitt, John Tudor, Alan Kennedy, Jimmy Smith, David Craig, Tommy Cassidy and Frank Clark.

the hard way. Instead of winning at home, the lads got through every time away with Malcolm Macdonald scoring in every round.

It took no fewer than nine matches for United to get to Wembley which showed the tenacity of the side. Yet it all started insignificantly. A home draw with non-league Hendon in the third round and a home draw with small fry Scunthorpe in the fourth, both 1–1, looked distinctly embarrassing. Fortunately the replays were won by decisive margins (4–0 and 3–0) to set the away pattern. It was, however, the fifth round match at West Bromwich which saw United take off with an emphatic 3–0 win. The Geordie hordes besieged the Hawthorns in their thousands to out-shout and overpower the Albion fans. John Wile, a Durham lad, said it was more like playing away than at home and that's what it must have seemed like

to all the West Brom players.

Fans remember this game in preference to others in the competition because to them it represented 90 minutes of sheer skill and enterprise. United lost their play-maker Terry Hibbitt in the 18th minute with a groin strain but it made no difference. Jinky Smith was the sub and he had one of his special days. Albion eventually went down to goals from Macdonald, Tudor and Barrowclough.

The crowd of 42,760 at the Hawthorns seemed quite manageable compared with the 54,500 who came to St James's to watch Newcastle United v. Nottingham Forest in the sixth round. The fans remember that game too, but for another reason: it was to result in an FA inquiry.

That particular match has gone down in history as the 'riot game' or 'the match that never was' because

TERRY HIBBITT shows his elation at the Hillsborough win.

AND so does Terry McDermott.

it was eventually declared null and void. Riot, I felt, was too strong a word for what actually happened but nonetheless the stupid actions of the hooligans who charged from one end of the pitch to the other bringing the game to a standstill and banishing the players to the dressing-room did United no favours. Instead it brought the wrath of the authorities down around their heads.

This is what happened. United were trailing 3–1 and one of the players, Paddy Howard, had been sent off, so they were down to 10 men. Play was stopped when the fans invaded the pitch and the referee, Gordon Kew, took the players into the dressing-room. At that moment, Wembley seemed a million miles away.

After an eight-minute break the ref asked both managers if they wished to continue. Both said, 'Yes!' Forest, in fact, fell over themselves to get back onto the Park and who can blame them? The game was

deep into the second half, they had a 3–1 lead, and 11 men were playing against 10. But they reckoned without the spirit of the black-and-whites, not to mention a howling Cup-thirsty crowd.

A penalty struck home by McDermott gave hope to players and fans alike and suddenly United were alight. Tudor equalised at 3–3 and, amid great emotion, skipper Moncur scored the winner. Four goals to three, and the impossible had happened. Or had it?

In the Newcastle boardroom there were the usual after-match pleasantries. Forest chairman Mr J. H. Willmer, congratulated his opposite number, Lord Westwood, on a stirring victory and then a little later as he was leaving shouted across the room from the door: 'All the best in the next round—see you at Wembley.' No hassle, no words of doubt or reproach about the hold-up. Just the normal formalities. But once Forest had time to think things over they changed their minds and 24 hours later they lodged an appeal with the FA demanding a replay. Their case was that the so-called 'riot' had intimidated their players and caused them to lose concentration.

Oh, yes? Why was Forest boss Allan Brown so anxious to restart the game if his players were intimidated and why did the Forest chairman congratulate United on their victory after the game without giving any hint of an impending appeal?

No, Forest were beaten fair and square as far as I'm concerned but while their actions might have upset some United fans I don't blame them for what they did. That's football—if there's a chance you must take it. All professionals in the game realise that, and Forest were just using the law to their advantage.

The FA upheld their appeal and United had to go back into battle on a neutral ground—Goodison Park, this time. The replay ended 0–0 after extra time. Three days later both teams returned to Goodison and this time they were separated by a solitary Macdonald goal.

Semi-finals are nerve-wracking affairs. Victory seems so close yet so far away, your dreams about to be shattered or gloriously fulfilled. United met Burnley at Hillsborough's magnificent stadium in what turned out to be the tale of two Macs— Macdonald and McFaul. They did more than anyone to push United those final few yards along the path to Wembley.

SuperMac stole the headlines, of course, and his two classic goals are still the most frequently

MANAGER Joe Harvey, a seasoned Cup campaigner, shows 19-year-old Alan Kennedy round Wembley before the final with Liverpool, a club Alan was later to join.

UNITED players inspect the Wembley pitch.

MILBURN

Newcastle United Football Club

DINNER

To Celebrate the

F.A. CHALLENGE CUP FINAL TIE 1951

at the

SAVOY HOTEL
W.C. 2.

SATURDAY, 28th APRIL, 1951

Newcastle United Football Club

DINNER

To Celebrate the

CHALLENGE CUP FINAL TIE 1952

at the

SAVOY HOTEL
W.C.2.

SATURDAY, 3rd MAY, 1952

E. Milburn

Newcastle United Football Club

FOOTBALL ASSOCIATION
CHALLENGE CUP FINAL

Record

Celebration Dinner

AT

SAVOY HOTEL
W.C. 2

SATURDAY, 7th MAY, 1955

Chairman
MR. STAN SEYMOUR

—

1910 ★ 1924 ★ 1932 ★ 1951 ★ 1952

TERRY MCDERMOTT, now with Liverpool, cuts out a ball meant for Steve Heighway.

requested ones on Tyne Tees Television. After a goalless first half in which there wasn't a paper width between the teams Macdonald displayed all his awesome power to break Burnley's back. He scored once with Colin Waldron clinging to him like a limpet—Malcolm should have given him his shirt if he wanted it that badly—and another where speed of thought and foot brought him the desired reward. Tudor hooked the ball from the edge of United's penalty area towards the left wing, Hibbitt saw that Burnley's defence was wide to the wall and moved it forward first time, and there was Macdonald gallop-

ing through to beat the keeper.

But if Macdonald was magnificent so was McFaul. It would have been easier to blow out a light bulb than beat Willie that afternoon. He must have broken more than a few Claret hearts with the quality of his saves. The final whistle brought rare scenes of elation with moist-eyed Newcastle players saluting the bank of black-and-white-scarfed fans who had spent hard-earned cash to travel to Watford (for the Hendon replay), Scunthorpe, West Bromwich, Liverpool (twice) and finally Sheffield in their determination to see their heroes triumph. Harvey was out on the field

another in Laburnum Terrace and all three had gone on to win the coveted Player of Year award. Watching him made me realise that for every winner there must be a loser.

Wembley '74 was a rare experience for me, not only because Newcastle United were beaten for the first time on that hallowed turf but because I felt real humiliation at our performance. All the joys of the build-up evaporated on the day itself.

As an old Newcastle Cup warrior, I seemed to spend most of the period between the semi-finals and the Final giving TV and radio interviews and I kept saying: 'The pot's ours.' To a certain extent it was just bravado because I considered Liverpool to be the best team in the land but it was good propaganda and I had a genuine belief in Newcastle's Cup-fighting tradition. Once there, history could take over.

I met Bill Shankly just before the final and he said: 'I've listened to what you've been saying, Jackie. And I admire you for it—you have to support your club. But, Jack, you *know* what's going to happen!' Shanks was a born winner!

United had lost right-back David Craig with a dislocated elbow and Joe moved Frank Clark to the other flank bringing in Alan Kennedy, at 19 the youngest player on the field. Jimmy Smith was chosen in preference to Stewart Barrowclough at No 7 and Tommy Gibb, who had played only in the third-round matches, was substitute to the following side: McFaul; Clark, Kennedy; McDermott, Howard, Moncur; Smith, Cassidy, Macdonald, Tudor, Hibbitt.

Before the kick-off there was a race round Wembley involving several well-known athletes and Brendan Foster, a Newcastle fanatic running in a black-and-white striped vest, destroyed the field to rapturous applause from the happy Geordie fans. What we didn't realise was that we should all have gone home then. What followed belonged to a different league.

United were dreadful. They somehow managed to keep the score to 0–0 by half-time but the second-half was a walk-over. After Alec Lindsey has seen a goal chalked off Kevin Keegan got a couple and Steve Heighway another to make the scoreline 3–0. I was so embarrassed I tried to hide. It's not often I've been ashamed of the Magpies, but I was saddened and shocked by the performance. Only the goalkeeper and the full-backs played. The rest were rubbish. Macdonald had been shouting from the rooftops as

with his troops clapping his hands, his face wreathed in smiles at the thought of going back to Wembley.

It was a wonderful moment for anyone with black-and-white eyes but I'll never forget, either, the dignity of a Geordie who couldn't join in the celebrations. I refer of course to Burnley manager Jimmy Adamson who behaved magnificently and put on a brave face but I could see the heartache in his eyes. Here was a man who, as a player and a manager, had brought great credit to my home town of Ashington. He and my cousin's lads, Bobby and Jackie Charlton, were born within three doors of one

usual about what he was going to do but the only thing he did that afternoon was tie his bootlaces. Jinky was at his worst—and subbed. It was awful. I could see Joe's face and he was looking sicker with every minute. Poor Joe! what dreadful humiliation for such a magnificent Cup performer to suffer!

Terry McDermott dissappointed us all at Wembley but he must have found it difficult playing against a team from his home town. Once he moved to Liverpool he became a first-rate player, and went on to play for England too. There's no doubt in my mind that you put a little extra in your performance when there's local honour at stake.

For skipper Bob Moncur, Wembley was a sad finale. He never kicked another ball for the Club and went down the road to Sunderland. He lacked pace, did Bob, but he had an old head on his shoulders and he did a captain's job in the sleeves-rolled-up way of his boss. He deserved a better send-off.

The only winners—apart from big Bren—were the fans. They were superb throughout and did a lot to try and raise Newcastle's game. Even as the beaming Emlyn Hughes mounted the stairs to the Royal Box and strode forward to receive the Cup chants of

'United, United' echoed round the stadium. Unbelievable.

But once the players had disappeared down the tunnel, disappointment and humiliation swept over Newcastle fans and for the first time in my life I saw scores of them throwing away their black-and-white scarves as they trudged wearily home.

Geordies, I need hardly tell you, are a resilient race and 24 hours later they were back on top. There was some pride to be gleaned from finishing second out of 92 Football League clubs plus the smattering of non-League outfits which had entered the FA Cup. They clung on to that pride and the home-coming for a side which had hardly crossed the halfway line in 90 minutes was out of this world.

United's players just wanted to creep into the Central Station. In fact they even asked if the home-coming arrangements and open-topped coach to take them round the city and up to St James's could be cancelled because they felt no one would turn up to see them. As it happened thousands lined the route and thousands more crowded into the Park. They were treated like heroes and reduced to tears and promises of redemption. In some ways I wish the homecoming

could have happened before the final and made them realise they were playing for the best folk in the world.

Shanks has told me more than once that only two sets of fans ever out-shouted Liverpool at Anfield and they belonged to Newcastle and Sunderland. He had a great admiration for the North East. 'If ever an area deserves success it's Tyne and Wear—in that order,' he said.

On a more personal note the final produced an extra disappointment for me and the rest of the lads who had won the Cup three times in the 1950s. With the exception of George Robledo who was back home in Chile, the whole team had met up again for my testimonial match some months earlier and we had recaptured that magic spirit so well we vowed to

JOHN TUDOR gets in a header at the Liverpool goal.

STEVE HEIGHWAY leaves Bob Moncur in his wake.

65

UNITED'S players leave the Central Station on an open-topped bus on their return home.

Howway the lads!

NORT

66

HOWWAY THE LADS
NEWCASTLE UNITED
1973 - 1974

The Journal
Well done the lads!

SKIPPER Bob Moncur holds up a mock Cup to the faithful fans at St. James's.

repeat the experience. Wembley under Joe Harvey seemed the ideal opportunity. But the Club didn't invite their old players to the final or the banquet afterwards even though Liverpool wined and dined their former stars. It hurt us all deeply, especially as we had achieved more than Liverpool's ex-players.

I was at Wembley in my capacity as a Press man but most of the other lads missed out completely. It wasn't that we wanted something for nothing—I'm certain that all of us would gladly have paid to have been part of the big day. I hope United don't forget the next time.

Despite the Cup Final flop and all the gloom I still maintain that at the time Joe Harvey was only two players away from having a great side. There was plenty of talent in the team and a couple of truly inspired players like, say, Keegan, Gemmill or Souness, would have had a lot of influence on the rest and generally heightened the standard. Joe was very close indeed to giving Newcastle United supporters what they wanted during his reign as manager.

A sea of faces—United's fans welcome back the team after the '74 Cup final.

JOE HARVEY is chaired by enthusiastic supporters.

WEMBLEY WILLIES

Part Two

TWO years after the Liverpool drubbing Newcastle were back at Wembley. This time it was for the League Cup final which, although lacking the magic of the FA Cup, has nonetheless established itself in recent years as a showpiece game. Within that short space of time United had acquired a new manager and virtually a new team. Gordon Lee was the boss now and only Alan Kennedy, Pat Howard, Tommy Cassidy and Malcolm Macdonald remained from the FA Cup side.

Bob Moncur had donned the red-and-white stripes, Terry McDermott had signed for Liverpool for £166,000, Terry Hibbitt had gone to Birmingham for £100,000 and Jim Smith and John Tudor were crippled by knee injuries. Before retiring, Joe Harvey had brought in Glen Keeley (Ipswich), Micky Burns (Blackpool), Geoff Nulty (Burnley), Tommy Craig (Sheffield Wednesday) and Mike Mahoney (Torquay) while Lee had added Alan Gowling (Huddersfield) and John Bird (Preston).

The Wembley trail began with a six-goal thrashing of Southport who had sacrificed home advantage for the financial gains of playing at St James's. The goals were shared by Gowling (4) and Paul Cannell (2). Cannell, playing instead of the injured Macdonald, was a strictly limited striker: good in the air, happy to dish out a bit of stick, but never capable of capturing the imagination. He eventually took his Geordie grit over to the States and did very nicely, thank you.

Bristol Rovers were dispensed with 2–0 at the Park after a 1–1 draw in the West Country and then came a

AT Wembley—Glen Keeley, Ray Blackhall, Paul Cannell, Tonny Cassidy, manager Gordon Lee, Steward Barrowclough and Alan Gowling.

MICKY BURNS, who enjoyed a great League Cup final, holds off Manchester City's Dennis Tueart.

GOAL—Alan Gowling equalises for Newcastle United.

super 3–1 win over QPR with Nulty, Burns and Macdonald scoring the goals. Strangely, that was the only goal SuperMac scored in the League Cup that season. A scrambled 1–0 home victory over Notts County, with Notts keeper Eric McManus kindly scoring an own-goal on our behalf, eased United through to the semi-finals and an instant sniff of the big time.

Spurs were next on the list and United, keeping it tight at White Hart Lane, came away only one goal to the bad. If 49,902 folk had any doubt (and Geordies believe their team can walk on water this close to Wembley) then that doubt was dispelled as Pat Jennings hesitated fatally coming off his line in the opening minutes and a galloping Gowling stroked the ball home to level the aggregate. Further goals by Nulty and Keeley made it 3–1 on the night and 3–2 overall.

The victory was particularly sweet because the London Press, in their usual way, had predicted that the Tottenham cockerel would be crowing at our national stadium that February and had travelled up en masse to witness their mob do the deed. They weren't happy at being proved wrong—especially by the northern boys.

Although Jennings had an off-day in the semi-final I rate him one of the best keepers in the world. And I'll let you into a secret—he should have been playing for Ipswich Town, not Spurs or Arsenal. When I was manager of Ipswich a local Irish scout called Jimmy Donnolly was onto me for weeks imploring me to go over and get a kid from Newry called Pat Jennings. But I was too involved trying to breathe life into an ailing club to do anything about it. I missed out on a gem. Jimmy had been my accountant in Belfast when I was playing for Linfield and he certainly knew the game. The only other player he ever recommended to me at Ipswich was a ginger-haired lad from Glentoran who later went to Stoke City. His name: Terry Conroy, an Eire international whom Joe Harvey tried to bring to United at the height of his career. The problem was that Jimmy had never scouted for a League club before and, being desperately busy anyway, I didn't take him seriously enough. A lesson to all managers and chief scouts.

1976 was a good year for Newcastle at least as far as cup competitions were concerned. Five days before they went to Wembley for the League Cup final against Manchester City they beat Bolton at the third attempt to reach the sixth round of the FA Cup and

UNITED'S tired players, led by Alan Gowling, salute their fans at the end of the League Cup final.

foster thoughts of a unique double Wembley appearance in the same season.

However Bolton inadvertently cost United dearly. During the first meeting at Burnden Park, in which Macdonald scored two of the most breathtaking goals of his career to earn United a 3–3 draw, keeper Barry Siddall accidentally broke Geoff Nulty's jaw with as powerful a hook as Rocky Marciano ever threw. United had already reached the League Cup final and that blow, as Nulty challenged for a cross Siddall attempted to punch out, cost the ex-Burnley man the glory of captaining a side at Wembley.

Instead that honour went to Nulty's best mate Tommy Craig and the spare place in the side was claimed by Stewart Barrowclough, who had just been edged out of the FA Cup final in 1974. The team consisted of: Mahoney; Nattrass, Kennedy; Barrowclough, Keeley, Howard; Burns, Cassidy, Macdonald, Gowling, Craig (T). Sub: Cannell.

The build-up was all against United. They played Bolton at Elland Road in the FA Cup on the Monday of Wembley week without Macdonald who was unfit and, though they won 2–1, the players were exhausted after such a tough match. Then during the week they began to go down like ninepins with a 'flu bug which started with Nattrass being subbed during the Bolton replay and ended with Gowling succumbing a few hours after the Wembley final.

Forty-eight hours before the final only five players were fit enough to make the journey to the capital.

When Alan Gowling equalised an early Peter Barnes goal following a Macdonald-Cassidy build-up it genuinely seemed possible that United could cause an upset but Dennis Tueart blew all that with his famous scissor-kick winner shortly after the interval.

United courageously took the play to City in the last half hour with Micky Burns knocking the ball round particularly well. Credit must be given to Gordon Lee for getting the best out of Burns during his time at Newcastle. Micky is a single-minded little fella who had been suspended by United prior to Lee's arrival and looked more likely to be on his bike than playing in a Cup final. But Lee released Burns from a strict touchline role and gave him the same freedom Bob Stokoe had allowed him at Blackpool. Burns operated just behind front runners Macdonald and Gowling where his natural goal sense was used to its best advantage.

Out of the 1976 Cup side I must admit to a particular liking for one player, captain Tommy Craig. I've always been impressed by his sheer ability and class, like that of his fellow left-footer, Hibbitt. Tommy first caught my eye in an England–Scotland Under 23 international at St James's Park when I thought he outshone England's Alan Hudson. At that time all other managers were raving about Hudson so I was well chuffed when Harvey bought Craig to replace Hibbitt at a time when Terry was sidelined with a knee injury. It was a great shame that Tommy became involved in the player power struggle which marked a sour period of United's history under Gordon Lee and Richard Dinnis. Unlike other key figures he was never a politician by nature but probably soiled his reputation on Tyneside by throwing in his lot with the aggressors.

It would have been nice if Tommy had got his hands on the League Cup but a week later the glory game was all over for another year as United went to Derby County in the sixth round of the FA Cup with a patched-up side and got turned over 4–2. Apart from Nulty they were also missing Mahoney, Nattrass and Craig himself while their third choice keeper, Eddie Edgar, was making his debut on that occasion. Two other new kids, Bomber Blackhall and Rocky Hudson, completed the team.

But there was still one more fling—in Europe, not at Wembley—before United slid alarmingly from their lofty perch in the First Division as a direct result of managerial chaos and player power.

The rest were still tucked up with a thermometer and a bottle of medicine hoping to make the trip later. It was a pathetic little party, already shorn of Nulty and with Nattrass carrying a bad knee injury as well as a heavy cold. Actually Nattrass should never have played. He underwent a fitness test in the grounds of United's Cockfosters hotel on the Saturday morning but, with the knee heavily bandaged, his movement was severely restricted. His game is all about pace, ease on the ball, and attacking flair on the overlap yet he never once ventured over the halfway line against City.

Nonetheless there was, thankfully, no humiliation for United this time round. Far from it. Although some of the players were still suffering the after-effects of 'flu they performed admirably and City had their work cut out.

OTHER CUP WINS

ARTEMIO FRANCHI, the president of UEFA, hands skipper Bob Moncur the Anglo-Italian Cup after United had beaten Fiorentina 2–1 in Italy in 1973.

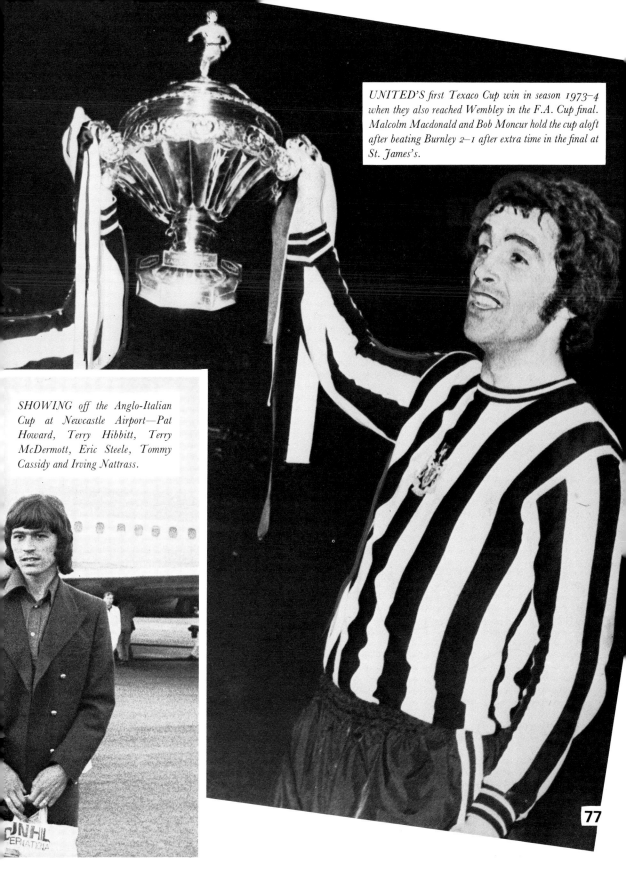

UNITED'S first Texaco Cup win in season 1973–4 when they also reached Wembley in the F.A. Cup final. Malcolm Macdonald and Bob Moncur hold the cup aloft after beating Burnley 2–1 after extra time in the final at St. James's.

SHOWING off the Anglo-Italian Cup at Newcastle Airport—Pat Howard, Terry Hibbitt, Terry McDermott, Eric Steele, Tommy Cassidy and Irving Nattrass.

UNITED *retain the Texaco Cup in 1974–5 beating Southampton in a two-legged final. Standing (left to right) : Frank Clark, Alex Bruce, Paul Cannell, Malcolm Macdonald, John Tudor, Ray Hudson. Front : Micky Burns, Alan Kennedy, Irving Nattrass, Iam McFaul, Pat Howard and Dennis Laughton.*

ALAN KENNEDY shows off the trophy to the fans on a lap of honour.

THE Saints are beaten and it's time to show off the spoils.

79

BACK IN EUROPE

UNITED failed to earn themselves a return journey to Europe until 1977, seven long years after their last Fairs Cup appearance. Rather to everyone's surprise they finished fifth in the First Division that year, but behind the scenes the rot had already set in. Gordon Lee, who masterminded the team's successful League Cup run, was lured away to Everton and he was immediately replaced by first-team coach Richard Dinnis. His appointment was largely the result of pressure from senior players who failed to understand that Dinnis had little experience of managing a team at this level. As a result United's first foray into the UEFA Cup wasn't the glittering affair we might have hoped for.

Given their current form, the team were lucky to be drawn against the Bohemians, part-timers from Dublin, as opposed to some more prestigious European side. United came away with a 0–0 draw from Dalymount Park, home of Eire's international side, after a match memorable for its displays of political religious bias rather than the quality of its football.

Newcastle goalkeeper Mike Mahoney was felled by a brick thrown from the roof of the stand behind his goal, after which a misguided United supporter raised a Union Jack in the face of the Tricolour. All hell broke loose. The trusty weapon of the street fighter—the brick, began to fly. You'd think that police reinforcements would have been brought in. Not a bit of it. There was nobody to stop the Bohemians' supporters hurling stones onto the pitch and eventually

WE'RE there—Newcastle United celebrate finishing fifth top of the First Division, their highest placing for years, and their qualification for the UEFA Cup. (left to right) ; Manager Richard Dinnis, Mike Mahoney, Alan Kennedy, Paul Cannell, Tommy Cassidy, Tommy Craig, Aidan McCaffery, Geoff Nulty, Stewart Barrowclough and Ray Blackhall. Front: Alan Gowling, Graham Oates, Micky Burns.

PLAYERS and officials gather round goalkeeper Mike Mahoney after he had been felled with a bottle in the tie against Bohemians in Dublin.

the players were taken off the field for 11 minutes until things quietened down.

It was a sickening business and the Bohs, thoroughly ashamed by their supporters behaviour, failed to produce any fireworks in the return leg. They surrendered 4–0 at St James's to a couple of goals apiece from Alan Gowling and Tommy Craig. Despite this defeat, two Bohemian players—full-back Fran O'Brien and winger Gerry Ryan—greatly impressed Dickie Dinnis, who praised them publicly. It began to look as if a transfer deal was in the air.

But something wasn't quite right. About an hour before the start of the return match at St James's, Tommy Docherty, then boss of Derby County, breezed in through the door and immediately I thought: 'Hello, what's off here?' ... Normally when two old pros like Tommy and myself get together you can't get a word in edgeways but on this occasion the Doc, one of the best patter merchants around, was strangely quiet and distant. He made a few desultory remarks but I could tell his mind was miles away. I knew the Doc was up to something.

After the match Newcastle's directors were running about like scalded cats and it was obvious that

transfer business was cooking. O'Brien and Ryan were shepherded into the drinks' room followed by an intense-looking Dinnis ... and all the time Tommy Doc stood impassively in the foyer. Saying nothing.

Eventually a double transfer deal was all tied up and the Bohs set off for their city centre hotel with a promise that the two players would return to the Park the following morning to sign the forms. United's directors appeared well pleased with themselves. At this stage the Doc, still saying nothing, left the ground. Only he didn't go straight home to Derby: instead he went down to the Bohs' hotel, booked himself in for the night, and summoned the Irish officials to a meeting.

In his Manchester United days Tommy had done a load of deals in Ireland where he had a good reputation and anyway the man is totally irrepressible. Soon he'd agreed terms with Bohemians and it was left to the players to decide between Derby and United. There was no contest. The next morning, with newspapers carrying the news of United's capture, O'Brien and Ryan took a taxi up to St James's to tell Dinnis it was all off. They then flew by private plane to Derby. Even though O'Brien failed a medical and

82

didn't sign, Ryan did and United looked stupid.

It was a classic case of the 'pro' beating the 'amateur'; Docherty out-doing Dinnis. In fact schoolmaster Dickie, without a footballing background, found it almost impossible to break into the transfer market to halt United's slide towards disaster and eventually he had to ask chairman Lord Westwood, who had tremendous contacts in Scotland, to help him.

Dickie did complete one transfer on his own, Dennis Martin from Carlisle for £40,000, but frankly Bob Moncur was more chuffed about that than Newcastle fans!

Though both Blackley and Martin were signed in early October neither had arrived inside the time limit for the second round of the UEFA Cup when United were paired with Bastia, on Napoleon's island of Corsica.

In fact United did reasonably well against Bastia, nicking an early goal through Paul Cannell to lead at half-time. Although they eventually lost 2–1 they fought to the end and the match was always in doubt. A 1–0 win at home would be enough to get through on away goals.

Bastia's big name was Johnny Rep, who had been a

ARMS raised, Alan Gowling shows his delight at opening the scoring in United's 4–0 second leg win over Bohemians at St. James's.

regular member of Holland's successful World Cup side in 1974. Rep was supposed to be carrying an injury in the first leg and he never kicked a ball which prompted Tommy Craig to make the unfortunate remark that Rep was the most unimpressive world-class player he'd ever seen. Maybe so, but in the second leg Rep struck—bang, bang—and United were out on their ear. He scored two thunderous goals of genuine quality in a 3–1 victory for Bastia.

Rep showed the same excitement in his strikes as Malcolm Macdonald and for weeks those lucky enough to be in the 35,607 crowd talked of SuperMac's return to Tyneside 'for the wrong flippin' side'.

United's plight was underlined by the fact that they fielded no fewer than 18 players in their four European ties including the likes of Ralph Callachan, David McLean, Peter Kelly, Ray Blackhall, Aidan McCaffery and Steve Hardwick plus a far-from-fit Geoff Nulty.

Within a very short time of Bastia's hammer blow Dinnis was sacked and the whole sorry episode wrapped up.

SKIPPER Geoff Nulty exchanging pennants before the start of the UEFA Cup tie against Bastia in Corsica.

JOHNNY REP, the Dutch World Cup star who was to destroy United in the return leg, wriggles away from his markers Alan Gowling and Tommy Craig during Bastia's home match.

UNITED'S best-ever modern side according to Jackie Milburn—the 1961 F.A. Cup winning team. Back row (left to right): Bobby Cowell, Joe Harvey, Frank Brennan, Jack Fairbrother, Bobby Corbett, Charlie Crowe. Front row: Tommy Walker, Ernie Taylor, Jackie Milburn, George Robledo, Bobby Mitchell.

THE 1955 Cup squad. Back row (left to right): Jimmy Scoular, Tommy Casey, Bobby Cowell, Ronnie Simpson, Jackie Milburn, Bob Stokoe, Ron Batty, Charlie Crowe. Front row: Manager Dugald Livingstone, Len White, Reg Davies, Vic Keeble, Ivor Broadis, George Hannah, Bobby Mitchell, trainer Norman Smith.

UNITED'S *team of the early 60's in the new strip with 'petticoat' shorts. Back row: Dick Keith, Brian Wright, Dave Hollins, Bill Thompson, Alf McMichael, Jackie Bell. Front row: Billy Day, Jimmy Kerray, Barrie Thomas, Ivor Allchurch, Jimmy Fell.*

JOE HARVEY'S *United in season 1973–4 when they went on to reach the F.A. Cup final. Back row: Martin Burleigh, Stewart Barrowclough, Tommy Gibb, Irving Nattrass, Iam McFaul. Middle row: manager Joe Harvey, David Craig, Gordon Hodgson, Tommy Cassidy, Pat Howard, Jim Smith, Terry McDermott, coach Keith Burkinshaw. Front row: Malcolm Macdonald, Bob Moncur, Frank Clark, John Tudor, Tony Green, Terry Hibbitt.*

UNITED *line up as follows: Back row: manager Gordon Lee, John Bird, Glen Keeley, Alan Gowling, Roger Jones, Mike Mahoney, Graham Oates, Irving Nattrass, Tommy Cassidy, coach Richard Dinnis. Front row: Micky Burns, Tommy Craig, Pat Howard, David Craig, Geoff Nulty, Steward Barrowclough, Alan Kennedy, John Tudor.*

UNITED *season 1980–81. Back row: Iam McFaul (coach), Nigel Walker, Ray Clarke, Billy Rafferty, Kevin Carr, Stuart Boam, Ken Mitchell, Steve Hardwick, Bobby Shinton, John Brownlie, Steve Carney, Geoff Allen (coach). Front row: Frans Koenen, Peter Cartwright, Ian Davies, Mick Martin, manager Arthur Cox, Terry Hibbitt, Peter Kelly, Alan Shoulder, Kenny Wharton.*

COMING CLEAN

LORD WESTWOOD, who carried on the great tradition of Newcastle United board by becoming Football League president

NEWCASTLE United have always been a 'clean' club in which illegal payments are almost unknown. United are proud of their close links with the Football League and have, over the years, produced a succession of Management Committee members including George Rutherford, Wilf Taylor and Lord Westwood. Indeed Lord Westwood, a former chairman held the highest office in soccer, that of Football League president, until March 1981.

It stands to reason that a club with so much pull in the corridors of power is not going to risk sullying itself by deliberately bending the rules. Can you imagine what it would have been like for Lord Westwood to have his Club hauled before the League for dropping players a few quid?

United must be seen to be whiter than white which makes things tough for a manager trying to pull off a big transfer or for players looking for a little extra. After all, they know that players at other clubs are getting it. It's no secret that several prominent clubs with a 'good' public image are not averse to rewarding their employees a bit more liberally than they should do. I'm not suggesting that they would stoop to fixing matches, but they certainly offer 'incentives', as they are termed.

Whenever I used to join up with the England squad during my playing days I would hear players from other clubs talking about 'programme money' and for a long time I wondered what on earth they were on about. Programme money, it turned out, was surplus cash raised by the clubs on match days, probably through the sale of the official programme, and then shared out among the players. I often heard that expression—but never at Newcastle where the chairman, George Rutherford, would have no hanky panky.

There was one occasion, mind you, when we all thought we'd cracked it. After one of our FA Cup final wins there was to be a celebration dance at the Oxford Galleries in the centre of town. Our wives were to be presented with handbags and, rumour had it, they would be stuffed full of cash. Fair dues, you might think, considering that we had made the Club rich through our endeavours.

Boy, did we look forward to the quickstep! Remember, a player's wage in those days was peanuts, he lived in a modest club house and travelled into training on the bus. Nothing fancy. Come the big night we all sat there trying to conceal our delight, as one by one our wives trooped up to the bandstand. The handbags they were given were bulging almost to obscene proportions and in fact the strap of Mrs George Hannah's bag snapped as she carried it back to her table. A dozen pairs of eyes registered the same thought: 'It's the weight. Whoopee!'

With a nonchalant air the lads remarked how beautiful the bags were then, hardly able to contain themselves, grabbed them and ripped them open.

Each one was stuffed with newspaper. Not a sign of the green crinkly stuff anywhere. Looking back, we must have been quite a sight sitting up to our knees in crumpled newspaper, but I don't remember being particularly amused at the the time. To make matters worse we later learned that the Club had bought a job lot of about thirty bags for seventeen quid! Another time the Club planned to give us a legitimate reward in the form of a gold watch each but even then officialdom took a hand and the Football Association blocked it. Charming!

Don't get me wrong. We played for the glory and the love and I'd never swap what I achieved for the meaningless careers of some of today's money-grabbers, but as a stony broke family man in the days after the war anyone would have been a little envious of the perks floating about elsewhere in the game.

We were one of the best sides in the country in the early 1950s, and a hundred quid was ten week's wages to us but we once played in the FA Cup when the opposition were on £750 a man to beat us. They didn't, because our pride was on the line and we had something others hadn't: a crowd which genuinely loved us. You couldn't buy that with hard currency.

Call us naive but we came by a bit of extra jam in a more mundane way. For example, before our first Cup final in 1951 the players brought out a brochure and we put up trestles in the car park outside the ground and sold them ourselves at two bob each.

Imagine it—top First Division stars trying to flog souvenirs to the crowd before dashing off at half past two to get changed. What's more, we didn't sell half as many as we should because we would stand nattering to a fan instead of moving him on and getting to the next customer. Those were the days. We were hard up but we were happy.

A United Effort

PICKING the best Newcastle United side of the last 40 years is likely to give anyone an ulcer. We've had one or two special players wearing the black-and-white over the years and trying to whittle them down takes a bit of doing, believe me. So I've cheated.

Instead of picking one team I've picked three: one to entertain, one to win the Cup and one to win the League. And why not? It gave me three times as much fun and anyway I firmly believe it takes vastly different talents and different combinations of players to achieve different aims.

Of course I could have taken the easy way out and simply named the 1951 FA Cup team. That's the sort of faith and respect I have for those players. Instead I've chosen to take a long hard look at every Magpie who has taken to the wing since the war years.

First let's look at the 'Entertainers', each one 18 carat gold at the box office. In goal I would have no hesitation in selecting Ronnie Simpson because he stopped just as many shots with his feet as his hands. He was a goal-line keeper, with spectacular lightning reflexes. He had a habit of walking on the balls of his feet as though always ready to spring. The only thing which stops Ronnie getting in my best side is his lack of height which meant he never dominated the penalty area.

Given a 4–3–3 formation my right-back would be Irving Nattrass. He was majestic to look at and had a lot of pace for a defender although he was usually content to remain in second or third gear. At centre back I'd select two Scots who would terrify the opposition—John McNamee and Frank Brennan. You never quite knew with Mac whether he would score for you or the opposition and he was guilty of a certain clumsiness, but the crowd took him to their hearts. Brennan? Well, he was an actor as well as a king. He deserved an Oscar for the way he would hammer a forward to the ground then, as the referee appeared, pick him up full of concern and pat him on the head. Left-back must be Alan Kennedy, who would run through a brick wall just because he had a black-and-white shirt on. He was a crowd-pleaser if ever there was one with a superb left foot and

blistering pace though, he didn't tackle well for a defender.

In midfield I ran into trouble because there have been so many value-for-money fellas over the years. Yet in the end the three I've selected almost picked themselves.

How, for example, could you have an 'Entertainers' side without the Clown Prince of Soccer, Len Shackleton? Shack was the greatest ball player of all time. He could balance a football on a snowflake. He was a born entertainer and always original and inventive. Shack didn't know what he was going to do

THE Bobby Dazzler ... Bobby Mitchell, whose ball skills tormented the best full-backs in the First Division.

FRANK BRENNAN, the Rock of Gibraltar.

next, so what chance had us mere mortals playing with him?

On the right side of Shack I'd play Jimmy Smith, who could put the ball through the eye of a needle with his right peg. His nickname, Jinky, summed up his style perfectly. It was all mood with Jinky—if the mood was right he would murder a side but equally his couldn't-care-less attitude sometimes seeped through to his play and he could look the biggest fool around.

On the left I have no hesitation in going for Dougie Wright, who played with me just after the war. He had four cartilages out but always succeeded in slowing the game down to his pace and beating man after man through sheer skill. Dougie often used to feign throwing the ball one way, then throw it the other. He could always out-think the opposition.

Others I considered for midfield include golden boy Ivor Allchurch, little George Hannah, the precocious Alan Suddick, not to mention Terry Hibbitt and Tommy Craig. Some competition, don't you agree?

Up front SuperMac picks himself. It was worth the admittance money to hear him spout, even if he never kicked a ball. He was a man who made his own pressures and carried them effortlessly. I'd put Len White at his shoulder, with Bobby Mitchell to feed them both. White still has a big following on Tyneside and Mitch was old twinkle-toes himself. He destroyed the best right-backs in the land—Alf Ramsey, Ron Staniforth, the lot—often twice in one run.

So the Entertainers would take the field like this: Simpson; Nattrass, McNamee, Brennan, Kennedy; Smith, Shackleton, Wright; White, Macdonald, Mitchell. Sub: Suddick. Put them out as a team and the score would probably be 8–8. But the gates would be locked.

Now to the Cup, our special tournament, and in goal there could be only one man: Jack Fairbrother. He was the master when it came to angles and consequently he rarely had to throw himself around. The ball inevitably came to his chest. He practised to perfect his art and many's the time I've acted as his 'stooge', the attacker shooting on the run. He would tie a rope to the goalpost and give me the other end. As I ran in to smack a shot at him the rope would indicate exactly where Jack should be standing to take the shot. We'd work until the sweat was rolling down my back and Jack got his sums right. But I'll tell you something—Fairbrother was the only keeper I've

JOE HARVEY, the best skipper of them all.

known who I always felt would save any shot. And I've played for England with the likes of Frank Swift, Ted Ditchburn, and Bert Williams. Jack had one little fad. He insisted on playing in policeman's white gloves and used to go down to Market Street police station in Newcastle to get them. Perhaps that's how he directed the traffic so well!

My two full-backs would be Bobby Cowell and Frank Clark. Cowell was totally dedicated and a man who literally cried with frustration and anger every time we lost. He headed more shots off the line than

TONY GREEN, a magical little player cruelly robbed of a lasting impact at St. James's through injury.

TERRY HIBBITT, provider for SuperMac during the Harvey managerial reign.

94

MALCOLM MACDONALD the gladiator.

. . . and Supermac the cricketer.

GETTING in the picture—Macdonald and his partner John Tudor.

any other defender I can remember. I go for Clark as his partner because he had pace and very, very rarely got skinned though he wasn't really appreciated by the St James's crowd until he moved on to Nottingham Forest and helped them win the European Cup.

For sheer passion and that cup-tie atmosphere I can look no further than Joe Harvey and Frank Brennan at the centre of the defence. Running into Harvey was like hitting a bag of iron. He'd be my captain too, because although Bob Moncur did a good job in later years modelling himself on Joe there was only one Harv.

Brennan was an amazing man: 6ft 2½in and 14st yet he started off as a 2½lb baby. I've seen him eat 12 eggs and half a dozen rashers of bacon for breakfast with lashings of toast on top and then go straight out

and lead everyone in training. He was dubbed the Rock of Gibraltar and it was easy to see why. Once when we were playing cricket at Benwell he was running between the wickets when a wayward return headed straight for him. Big Frank never broke stride as he nodded the cricket ball down and completed his run laughing all over his face. That's the sort of teak-hard fella he was; a man who, unlike a lot of centre-halves, never squealed for cover. He'd tell his full-backs: 'Piss off out of the way and let me get on with the job.'

Frank never bothered much about appearances and I vividly remember him turning up for our tour of South Africa with a toothbrush in his top pocket and nowt else. He was presented with a Zulu spear the moment we arrived and Frank spent the entire 10 weeks travelling round the country with his tooth-

brush in one hand and his spear in the other. He borrowed shaving gear from me, vests from George Robledo, and socks from Mitch.

In midfield I'd bring together a selection of outstanding talent spanning the 1950s. First there's Ernie Taylor, 5ft 3in tall in his long studs. Ernie took size 4 shoes and used to get changed into his gear and pull on Brennan's boots over his own to trudge round the dressing-room like Coco the Clown. But on the Park he was a Mini with a Rolls-Royce engine. He could never last over 42 games but in the Cup he was sheer magic.

With Ernie I would partner the two Ivors, Allchurch and Broadis. Allchurch was a clever, scheming player with a good finish while veteran Broadis was strong on the ball and had good all-round skills. Few will forget the way he and Tom Finney

97

THE best of friends—Malcolm Macdonald embraces United keeper Mike Mahoney at the end of the game with Arsenal when Mac was returning to St. James's for the first time since his transfer and pulled in a bumper crowd.

FRANK CLARK enjoying himself Behind him is John Tudor.

WHERE did you get that hat. Classy full-back David Craig, a keen golfer like so many footballers.

GEORGE ROBLEDO and Jackie Milburn relax at a Turkish bath with singer Donald Peers.

IRVING NATTRASS, chasing the great Eusebio during a match at St. James's Park.

101

STAN ANDERSON signs for United watched by (left to right), secretary Dennis Barker, director Wilf Taylor and Sunderland manager Alan Brown.

destroyed the Scots at Hampden Park when they wore the white shirts of England.

Bearing in mind that I have a completely free hand in selecting this team and that it's wishful thinking anyway, I would love to lead the attack and, that being so, how could I possibly leave out my two front-line colleagues from 1951, namely George Robledo and Bobby Mitchell?

So, my Cup team is: Fairbrother; Cowell, Harvey, Brennan, Clark; Taylor, Allchurch, Broadis; G. Robledo, Milburn, Mitchell.

In the League I must go for stayers rather than sprinters and while not all the above players qualify on that score I would keep Fairbrother in goal but, after a lot of soul searching, switch my full-backs to bring in David Craig, a model of consistency and

class, and Ron Batty, who could cut wingers in two with his tackling. In that respect he was better than either Alf McMichael or Bobby Corbett.

For my money, Brennan would form part of any side but I might raise a few eyebrows by naming Bob Stokoe as his partner. When Bob was a promising right-half I tipped him to take over from Billy Wright in the England team but he was switched to the middle and subsequently lost a lot of his finesse. Nonetheless Stokoe was tremendously effective and possessed that quality so essential to Newcastle sides—he was black-and-white daft and hated losing. He still does . . . especially at golf.

Midfield sees me with four players for three positions. I've got to play Jimmy Scoular for his power, aggression and accurate passing. I must also go for

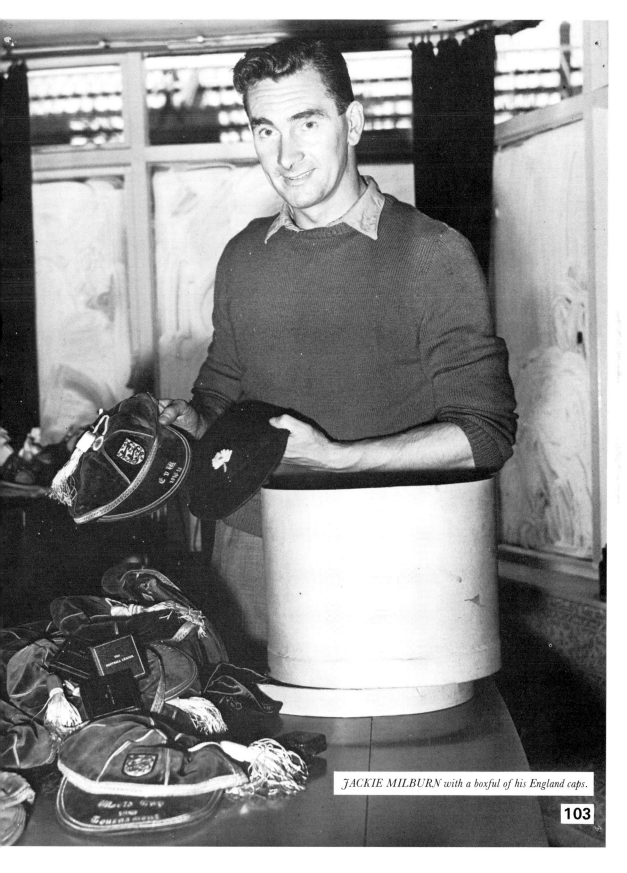

JACKIE MILBURN with a boxful of his England caps.

A unique picture of the England team in 1948 taken wearing their international caps before doing battle with Wales at Villa Park. Back row (left to right): Leuty, Scott, Aston, W. Winterbottom (manager), Swift, Wright, Ward, H. Bourne (trainer). Front row: Matthews, Mortensen, Milburn, Shackleton, Finney, Franklin.

IVOR ALLCHURCH, *Golden Boy of Welsh soccer.*

JACK FAIRBROTHER, *a goalkeeper with all the angles.*

JIMMY SMITH jinks round Liverpool and England centre-half Larry Lloyd.

GEORGE EASTHAM, an inside-forward of skill and poise.

RONNIE SIMPSON caught at his acrobatic best. A real entertainer.

ALAN KENNEDY who plays left-back with pace and power.   *IVOR BROADIS, who was capped by England.*

DEFENSIVE expertise from goalkeeper Jack Fairbrother and full-backs Bobby Corbett and Bobby Cowell in the 1951 F.A. Cup final against Blackpool.

TINY tot Ernie Taylor supports the F.A. Cup held by Joe Harvey. Ernie went on to play in Cup finals for Blackpool and Manchester United as well.

Tony Green, a fabulous maker and taker of chances whose injury was a tragedy to Newcastle. That leaves me with two men and one shirt to fill. Jim Iley was always a good player over a season but in the end I favour George Eastham, who to my mind was real England material. I played with Eastham on his Newcastle debut at Manchester United and we got caned 6–1 but he went on to delight Geordie fans for a while after that.

My attacking trio sees me indulge in another fantasy by teaming SuperMac with myself through the middle. If I needed anyone to feed our sprinting ability and our shooting power it would, of course, be Mitch who lasted season upon season without injury.

My League team then is as follows: Fairbrother; D. Craig, Stokoe, Brennan, Batty; Scoular, Eastham, Green; Milburn, Macdonald, Mitchell.

Seeing as we have to go 42 games I might be permitted a few 'reserves' in case of unforeseen accidents. That being the case I would put on stand-by players like Stan Anderson, who would have won more England caps with an extra injection of pace; Albert Stubbins, who would have been in all my teams if the war years hadn't interfered with his career; Pop Robson for his natural goal-scoring ability; and the classy Jim Iley.

No doubt the arguments are raging by now. How dare I leave out so-and-so? And what about Charlie Bloggs, a class player if ever there was one? Well, this great game of ours is all about opinion. That's what makes it so intriguing. There is no real answer to whether Malcolm Macdonald was a better centre-forward than Len White or Tony Green more skilful than Ernie Taylor. It's all in the eye of the beholder. But it's tremendous fun having your say, isn't it?

CONFRONTATION—big John McNamee, forever the tough man, challenges Spurs and Northern Ireland Goalkeeper Pat Jennings.

POP ROBSON, who began his League career with Newcastle United, is seen heading a goal against West Ham, ironically a club he was to join twice.

JIMMY SCOULAR, a mixture of toughness and skill.

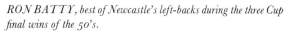
RON BATTY, best of Newcastle's left-backs during the three Cup final wins of the 50's.

ME AND MY FRIENDS

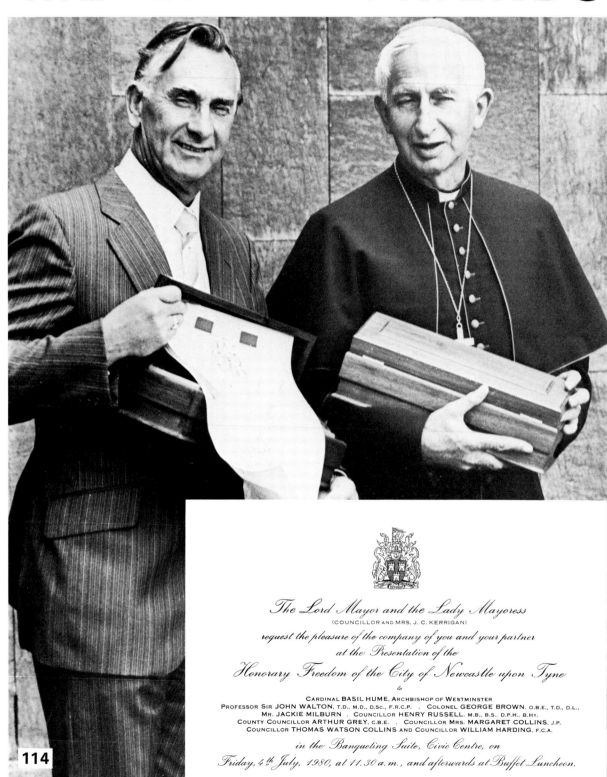

The Lord Mayor and the Lady Mayoress
(COUNCILLOR AND MRS. J. C. KERRIGAN)
request the pleasure of the company of you and your partner
at the Presentation of the
Honorary Freedom of the City of Newcastle upon Tyne
to

CARDINAL BASIL HUME, ARCHBISHOP OF WESTMINSTER
PROFESSOR SIR JOHN WALTON, T.D., M.D., D.SC., F.R.C.P. . COLONEL GEORGE BROWN, O.B.E., T.D., D.L.,
MR. JACKIE MILBURN . COUNCILLOR HENRY RUSSELL, M.B., B.S., D.P.H., B.HY.
COUNTY COUNCILLOR ARTHUR GREY, C.B.E. . COUNCILLOR MRS. MARGARET COLLINS, J.P.
COUNCILLOR THOMAS WATSON COLLINS AND COUNCILLOR WILLIAM HARDING, F.C.A.

in the Banqueting Suite, Civic Centre, on
Friday, 4th July, 1980, at 11.30 a.m., and afterwards at Buffet Luncheon.

PLEASE BRING THIS CARD WITH YOU

R.S.V.P. LORD MAYOR'S SECRETARY
CIVIC CENTRE . NEWCASTLE UPON TYNE NE1 8QA

114

ABOVE: In May, 1967, ten years after last playing for Newcastle United, Jackie Milburn was awarded a testimonial match at St. James's Park. A huge crowd of 45,404 turned up to pay tribute to Wor Jackie who brought together his old Cup mates and former stars as well as current internationals like Bobby and Jackie Charlton, Nobby Stiles and the legendary Ferenc Puskas.

HERE Jackie shakes hands with goalkeeper Jack Fairbrother as Joe Harvey looks on.

LEFT: Two great sons of Newcastle. Jackie Milburn and Cardinal Basil Hume, Archbishop of Westminster pictured after they had been made Freemen of the City in July, 1980.

ABOVE: From the same match. Milburn uses his trusty left foot as former Middlesbrough and Great Britain captain George Hardwick tries to intervene.

BELOW: Two great centre-forwards ... Wor Jackie and SuperMac.

TOP: *Gazing out over their beloved St. James's Park—Jackie Milburn and co-writer John Gibson, another self-confessed Newcastle United 'nut.'*

CENTRE: *Jackie Milburn's two famous relatives from Ashington, Bobby and Jackie Charlton wearing the white shirts of England.*

LEFT: *Jackie Milburn with Bobby and Jackie's mother Cissie Charlton talking to MP and television personality Clement Freud.*

117

MEETING for the annual selection of the Newcastle United Player of the Year are Tyne Tees Television's Alister Harrison, Jackie Milburn, Derek Teesdale, Evening Chronicle sports editor John Gibson and United manager Gordon Lee.

JACKIE MILBURN trying to live up to his initials of JET with Olympic medallist Brendan Foster, a Newcastle United supporter.

STAN SEYMOUR, Mr. Newcastle United.

Managing Fine or Otherwise

NEWCASTLE United never really bothered with managers until after the war but since then we've had a succession of them. Some have been colourful, some controversial, some good, some bad.

My first boss as such was George Martin, who joined us from Luton Town in May, 1947 on the strength of a gritty performance at Kenilworth Road when, after we'd been 3–0 up, they came back to win 4–3. That display of character by Luton impressed the Newcastle directors and Martin was duly imported. Actually, he was only the third manager in United's history following another Scot, Andy Cunningham, and Tom Mather but during his three-year stay he piloted us to promotion in 1948 and did me the great personal favour of converting me to centre-forward. I can't thank him enough for that.

How that momentous decision came about makes a good story. A bunch of us were sitting around having a natter: Stan Seymour, George Martin, Joe Harvey, our trainer Norman Smith and myself. The subject—surprise, surprise—was football and as Charlie Wayman had just departed we eventually got round to discussing who would take his place.

'Jackie's the man,' declared Martin.

'Naw, keep him at inside-left or on the wing,' said Norman, shaking his head.

'Aye, he's not good enough in the air for a centre-forward,' agreed Seymour.

I was nodding my head furiously in agreement. Remember, I didn't exactly shine in that position at school.

'They're right,' I said. 'I'm not cut out to lead the attack. I'm happy where I am.'

But Martin refused to wilt in the face of such mass opposition.

'You're wrong, all of you,' he said with conviction. 'I'll tell you something. Not only will Jackie make a centre-forward but he'll get a cap into the bargain.'

Sure enough, the boss got his way and, as I've already told you, in my first match as a No 9 the Bury keeper was carted off injured and I scored a hat-trick against his stand-in. Lucky? Maybe. But no one can deny that George Martin saw something a lot of us didn't because, far from being a one-match wonder, I went on to bag a few England caps just as he had prophesied. God bless his cotton socks!

George was a very likeable man whose main concern was the welfare of his players. In my day we all lived in club houses, not the four-bedroom detached jobs in the posh part of town which today's stars can afford, and George was always ready to help us get over any little financial difficulties. He would listen attentively if we reported a crack in the kitchen sink or in the ceiling and would get it repaired pronto. If he overheard me mention that Laura was ill he'd ring her up to ask how she was getting on. Attention to detail—that was his forte. He worked on the assumption that if you got the little things right then the big things would fall into place. Keep the wife happy and the husband will be free from worries and get on with his job.

On the Park we did the business for George right enough. He had a great singing voice, with which he would occasionally entertain the boys and in return we sang sweetly for him throughout the 1947–48 season, despite a succession of team changes. We sold star forwards like Roy Bentley, Len Shackleton, Charlie Wayman and Tommy Pearson; lost Tommy Walker, who broke an arm in training, and Bobby Corbett, who had a cartilage operation, and still finished in second place, three points behind Birmingham City. The chopping and changing is underlined by the fact that apart from Frank Brennan (42 appearances), me with 39 and Joe Harvey (37) not one player turned out in more than 26 of the 42 games. But promotion was clinched with Martin's signing, Frank Houghton, sewing things up nicely against Sheffield Wednesday in front of 66,483 fans. And in true black-and-white style it was an occasion to tug at the heartstrings. We were 2–2 with only three minutes to go when the courageous Houghton, a wing-half playing on the right wing, scored two goals and then promptly crashed into the goal post and broke his arm. As we trooped off the field to tumultuous applause George Martin was standing by the tunnel with both arms raised in the air. It was the proudest day of his life.

Martin departed in December 1950 to take up a similar post with Aston Villa and it was that old hand Stan Seymour who took us into the Wembley land of milk and honey. Actually Stan was always the big noise in the Club whoever else was around. He and Norman Smith virtually ran the squad between them

for most of my playing career, certainly during the glorious Cup-winning years.

Norman would give us a right rollicking in front of the directors and anyone else who cared to listen if we arrived back at the hotel after the 11pm deadline on away trips but he'd then take us round the back and buy us a half! He did his job well and we respected him for it.

Dougie Livingstone, the former Celtic and Aberdeen full-back, was a very different kettle of fish. He arrived in 1953 bristling with modern coaching techniques picked up in Sweden and proceeded to create more flak than a German panzer division.

Livingstone breezed in and turned training upside down. He had us jumping over high hurdles then ducking under them and leaping into the air to head the ball. After the first week there were no fewer than 10 players on the treatment table with groin strains. When we went to Sheffield United for our first game under the new Livingstone regime we lost by six goals with Jimmy Hagan, a Geordie we used to call The Stroller because of his style, tearing us to bits.

Frankly, we needed new training like a hole in the head. We had won promotion, attracting an average gate of 56,351 and lifted the FA Cup more than once. We were naturals and all the new techniques simply upset the balance. That at least was the view of the older players although some of the younger ones went along with the revolution and for the first time there was a rift in the club. Cliques began to appear.

Stan Seymour belonged to the old school and friction boiled up, as I have already mentioned, when Livingstone left me out of the 1955 Cup final side only to be over-ruled. Len White had been selected instead of me but when the directors reversed that decision Len still managed to make the final because poor little Reg Davies went down with tonsillitis.

This episode spelt the end of Livingstone. Fortunately he had made Joe Harvey coach for the 1955 Cup run and that saved us because he was able to bridge the gap between the senior players and the manager. We all thought the world of Joe and he used to say: 'Forget everything else. It's up to you lot on the field. You decide what really happens.'

Don't get me wrong in all this. I found Doug Livingstone a nice enough fella. It was his football methods that bothered me. When it came to what was best for the team our ideas were oceans apart.

My long playing association with United finally

DOUGALD LIVINGSTONE with Vic Keeble, Bobby Mitchell, Reg Davies, Jackie Milburn and Jimmy Scoular.

came to an end in 1957 when I joined the ranks of the managers. Understandably, people had come to expect rather a lot of me over the years. I was Wor Jackie, one of them, a pit lad who had made it to the dizzy heights and my self-imposed standards were extremely high. I'd always bust a gut to give them what they wanted but, at the age of 33, I was wondering how much longer I could keep going. There was no Harvey, Brennan, Robledo, Walker or Taylor now. Suddenly it wasn't the same team or the same atmosphere.

Just before his death the previous year my father told me: 'Get out while they remember you with affection. Don't spoil things.' That was after I'd played a game over in Ireland as part of the George Eastham deal and brought the house down. Linfield officials had loved me and they wrote asking if I fancied going across to Belfast as their player-manager.

Linfield, a part-time club, offered me a club house, £25 a week and a £1,000 signing-on fee which had some considerable attraction. My top whack with United as their England centre-forward was £17 a

week so I decided, with something of a heavy heart, to cut the ties and cross the Irish Sea.

United asked for £20,000 plus an inside-forward called Jimmy Hill (not the one on television) in exchange for me which I thought was pretty thick after my years of loyal service. They were skinning the club I was joining and consequently leaving no money in the Linfield coffers for me to buy new players.

All the same we cleaned up in my three years in Ireland. We won just about every domestic honour possible and I scored 150 goals from inside-left operating a lot deeper than in my heyday. Jackie Milburn even wrote himself a new line in the record books: I became a goalscorer in the relatively new European Cup!

As Irish League champions we played TFK Goteborg of Sweden in the European Cup in 1959 and 41,000 turned up at Windor Park to see us beat them 2–1 in the first leg. I scored both our goals but in the return they kicked me up in the air and we lost 6–1.

During my Belfast sojourn I also played for the

121

Irish League against the Football League at Blackpool. The opposition included 'foreigners' such as John White, Danny Blanchflower and Denis Law and though they beat us right enough I had a blinder and suddenly, at the age of almost 36, I found myself in demand again. I received a host of offers to return to the big time but, having drawn my £600 provident money, I was barred.

While I'd severed my playing connections with Newcastle United my love affair with them was as strong as ever. I regularly flew from Belfast to either Newcastle or London to watch United play and always paid the air fare out of my own pocket. They still meant that much to me.

Charlie Mitten, who became manager in June 1958, was one of the bosses who tried to get me back to England. He actually wrote to me suggesting I should re-sign for United which would have caused something of a stir had it been feasible. What a character he was. A very good outside-left in his playing days with Manchester United, he had a mania for buying outside-lefts at Newcastle in the hope of finding one better than himself. He even played his lad, John Mitten.

One of the first things he did on arriving at St James's was change the strip. He produced a new one with white edging on the shorts, thinner stripes and all white stockings with a black-and-white striped turn-down top. But it was the white edging on the shorts which caused all the fuss. When United ran out for their first away game in the new strip a voice bellowed from the paddock: 'Scoular, your bloody slip's showing!. One of the toughest wing-halves in the Football League winced visibly.

Mitten's gambling mania became something of a legend on Tyneside, and no wonder. A story, though never substantiated, has it that he once removed Len White from the treatment table so that one of his greyhounds, which was running at Brough Park that night, could have a bit of heat. And he was supposed to have installed a blower system in the manager's office to make it easier for him to keep up with the horse racing results.

Charlie the punter was much in evidence one day when I agreed to join United in Manchester before a League game against City. The only plane available at short notice was one travelling to Australia with a load of pigs but the pilot agreed to take me to Liverpool from where I could easily drop down the road into Manchester. So there was Jackie Milburn,

CHARLIE MITTEN, a real character.

sitting in the back surrounded by pigs as the pilot sang 'Three little girls sitting in the back seat' at the top of his voice.

When I arrived in Manchester Mitten was delighted to see me. Perhaps just a bit too delighted. He greeted me like a long lost brother and told the directors: 'Get the lads in the coach and off you go. We'll get a taxi to the ground later—I want to talk to Jackie.' In fact it turned out that he had a bet on the two o'clock race and wanted to watch it on telly. He'd just been wondering what excuse to give when I turned up and provided one for him.

I first saw Mitten's team in action at Arsenal and when I realised Bobby Mitchell was down to play left-half I nearly killed myself laughing. Mitch, a winger with a bit of a lazy streak playing left-half . . . crazy! But he was operating behind three of the finest inside-forwards in the game, namely Eastham, White and Allchurch and Mitch was a revelation. The best man on the field.

If the team looked good that day the dark clouds were still gathering. George Eastham refused to re-sign at the beginning of the 1960–61 season, eventually taking United to the High Court, and winning. By the end of the season Newcastle were relegated to the Second Division. Six months later Mitten was sacked.

United went down because they conceded a staggering 109 goals even though they scored 86, with White notching 28 in 33 games. I was at the game which many folk consider cost United their First Division status. It was at Tottenham and though Newcastle won 2–1 they lost the services of White for the remainder of their programme through injury.

Certainly Dave Mackay's tackle on White looked extremely nasty. Len was six yards from goal when he received the ball and anything could have happened. I could almost hear Mackay telling himself: 'I've got to stop him.' He launched himself at White and caught Len right across the back of the legs sending him crashing to the ground. What made it all look so bad was that Mackay appeared to be in mid-air for a good

five seconds before making contact. It was a shocker, all right, but overall I rated Mackay as a player. He virtually handed Brian Clough the First Division title at Derby County.

Mitten's departure in October 1961 and the subsequent dismissal of our old Cup trainer Norman Smith after a few months as stop-gap team manager opened the way for the return of Joe Harvey to St James's Park. His 13-year reign was to bring the club new-found success.

Joe's appointment in June 1962 came only 10 months before my move into the hot seat at Ipswich Town. After quitting Linfield and rejecting offers from Scottish clubs such as Partick Thistle I spent a season and a half as player-manager of non-league Yiewsley Town before landing the Ipswich job. Joe and I were on the phone to each other every day wallowing in gloom. United were heavily in debt and sinking fast towards the lower reaches of the Second

LOYAL UNITED fans travelled to Belfast to present Jackie Milburn with a special framed photograph after he had left Newcastle to become player-manager of Linfield.

Division. Meanwhile Ipswich were a First Division club with a Fourth Division team. We had no youth side and not a scout on the books.

I had succeeded Alf Ramsey, the idol of Ipswich, who was off to manage England and gain a knighthood for winning the World Cup. Alf lived in the town and visited the ground regularly, which didn't make me feel any better.

The first season I somehow managed to keep Ipswich afloat but the second year I couldn't prevent them from going down to the Second. Starting literally from rock bottom I wheeled and dealed and ended up flogging England centre-forward Ray Crawford to Wolves so that I could buy Gerry Baker, Joe Broadfoot, Frank Brogan and Danny Hegan for peanuts. I still reckon they were good purchases at the price but time was always against us.

A player is responsible for himself only, but a manager is in charge of everyone. Equally his future is in the hands of others and that can put an intolerable pressure on him. At Ipswich I felt the full force of that pressure and it got me down dreadfully. After yet another defeat I would sit in a darkened room, brooding for hours. For the one and only time in his life Jackie Milburn, virtually a non-drinker, turned to the bottle for solace. Without realising what I was doing I started drinking gin like it was going out of fashion. The side of my face even began to swell to grotesque shapes through worry after matches. It was all too much. Though I knew I was beginning to pull the club around and give it a firm foundation upon which to build, the physical demands were far too great and I resigned.

The response was immediate and, to a certain extent, reassuring, given my depressed state. The Ipswich players threatened to walk out if I were allowed to leave, which at least showed I had built up a sense of loyalty and communication. Then a national newspaper rang to offer me a job as a columnist back on Tyneside. What a lovely thought! Going home and being paid for it as well! I jumped at the opportunity.

While I was experiencing constant nightmares at Ipswich Joe was working through his problems at Newcastle. Mentally, Joe is probably tougher than I am. He is a man of iron will, a real Sergeant-Major who makes people jump. He doesn't take things to heart quite so much and that's essential if you want to survive in the managerial jungle.

Survive he did to pilot our old club to the Second

JOE HARVEY with his award after being voted Manager of the Month.

Division championship, the European Fairs Cup, the FA Cup final, a couple of Texaco Cup wins and the Anglo-Italian Cup, plus three lucrative years in Europe. In the process Harvey built three different teams, assembling the Second Division championship side around half-backs Anderson, McGrath and Iley, the Fairs Cup team around Davies and Robson and the Wembley side around SuperMac.

He took what he'd shown us on the pitch into the manager's office and added that special ingredient so vital to a boss: the ability to spot and sign real talent. Joe had two sides to him, the tongue-lasher and the lifter of sunken spirits. Such qualities are called 'man management'. Let me give you an example of both.

His first match as a player was against Blackpool at home. Within seconds of the start I pushed a ball back to him. It was a mile off the mark and went out of play. Now, I was working at the pits and I thought no one could teach a miner how to swear. But never in my life have I heard such a torrent of abuse. All the lads heard it, too, and got the message. Army man Joe

JOE HARVEY signs Terry McDermott from Bury. McDermott went on to play for Liverpool and England and be voted double Player of the Year for season 1979–80.

was in charge.

Players like Mitch, Tommy Walker and myself used to get a bit lax at times and we needed a touch of the verbals. On the other hand the likes of Charlie Crowe, Bobby Cowell and Ernie Taylor sometimes needed a boost and Joe psyched them up. I remember, for instance, Joe's comment to Ernie one day when the little lad was having a stinker. When Taylor had passed a decent ball Harvey stopped in mid-stride, placed his hands on his waist, and exclaimed: 'Ernie, there is not another man in the bloody game who could pass the ball like that.' You could see Taylor's chest puffing out and he was smartly back in the groove.

In management Joe sorted out his players in the same way. Terry Hibbitt, another little schemer supreme, walked into his office one morning without as much as a 'good day' and proceeded to have a natter about this and that before disappearing again happy as Larry. I asked Joe why he let him get away with it: most bosses insist on all players knocking on their door and waiting for a call to enter. 'Jackie,' said Joe, 'If it makes him feel good that's all right by me. All I want is for the little bugger to feel wanted and do his stuff on a Saturday.'

Malcolm Macdonald, perhaps Harvey's greatest signing, loved him like a father. 'I never had to ask for a rise in four seasons at Newcastle,' said Mac. 'Joe would just come up and say: "I got you a few more bob today, Mal" and there it would be in the next pay packet.'

Joe wisely surrounded himself with good men and two of his first-team coaches—Dave Smith from '68 to '71 and Keith Burkinshaw from '71 to '75—went on to become successful managers in their own right. Smith tasted promotion with both Mansfield Town and Southend United and Burky fashioned an exciting Spurs side buying Argentinian World Cup stars Ossie Ardiles and Ricardo Villa. No one, either, will forget the contribution made by Jimmy Greenhalgh to the promotion team.

Harvey's departure from the hot seat left a huge void and to fill it was obviously going to be a problem. Personally I've always wanted to see United appoint a Geordie boss, someone who understands this unique area and feels the passion we have for our football. Strangely, United haven't had a Geordie manager since the days when Stan Seymour and Norman Smith ran the ship—and look how successful they were. The nearest they have come was Harvey himself who became a naturalised Geordie. That's

THE passion and the strain is etched on the face of Joe Harvey as he shouts instructions from the St. James's dug-out.

FACING the Press. Gordon Lee smiles for the cameras.

why I was delighted when I was asked if I would discreetly 'sound out' Jackie Charlton to see if he would be interested in coming to St James's.

We've spawned a succession of highly successful managers such as Lawrie McMenemy, Bobby Robson, and Bob Paisley, as well as Jackie Charlton so it seemed only natural that one of them should come home and look after the black-and-whites.

The year was 1975 and Jackie was at Middlesbrough. I was given the task of approaching him because he's a relative—we could keep it in the family if you like. If he sounded interested an official approach could be made. But, incredibly, when I spoke to Jackie he told me he wasn't ready for such a big job yet. This from a man who a year before had won the Second Division championship by the length of Northumberland Street and been voted Manager of the Year. This from a brilliantly sound soccer judge

who had spotted Boro's weakness immediately and rectified it by signing Bobby Murdoch—and on a free transfer at that!

However Jackie's his own man and there's no changing his mind once it's made up. He'd been a Newcastle United fan as a kid and followed my career in every detail, in fact he used to come over to my house most Sundays to chat about the game, yet here he was turning down the chance to manage 'his' Club.

United now turned to Gordon Lee, a young manager who had won promotion from the Third Division with Blackburn Rovers, and thus entered one of the most controversial periods of their history. Lee's record on paper is good. In the two years he was boss at Gallowgate he took United to the League Cup final at Wembley and did all the spade work to prepare the side which qualified for Europe. But it

127

THE confrontation which rocked Tyneside. Gordon Lee (right) and the idol he sold, Malcolm Macdonald.

GORDON LEE and the man who succeeded him, Richard Dinnis.

was his dealings in the transfer market and his general soccer philosophy which first amazed and then angered Tyneside.

Lee walked into St James's Park and announced that from now on there would be no stars at Newcastle. Now this is just about the last thing in the world you should do up here. It's almost sacrilege to a crowd weaned on personality players to deprive them of their heroes and, in my opinion, it's downright silly. I've never ever gone along with the theory that one man doesn't make a team. One man does—often. Tom Finney carried Preston for years and to the punters Malcolm Macdonald *was* Newcastle United. But Lee sold SuperMac to Arsenal and also chucked out Terry Hibbitt. In their place he bought a succession of players from the Third Division he had just left. Alan Gowling was a success and John Bird must have had something for a person like Bobby

Charlton to resign over the transfer. But the rest! Graham Oates will always be remembered for the own goal he scored at the Gallowgate end, a 40-yard belter, which is more than can be said for the others who were instantly forgettable!

Looking back I don't blame Lee for selling Macdonald because Malcolm was thoroughly disillusioned and hadn't kicked a ball for a year but Lee must be blamed for doing that to United's star player. When SuperMac left something died on Tyneside and, perhaps, the rights and wrongs of the whole affair are summed up by the relative standing of both Gordon Lee and Malcolm Macdonald on Tyneside today. Only one is remembered with affection.

Lee wanted a team of grafters and there's no doubt that the players he surrounded himself with worked hard for him and achieved results. But the results came without excitement and that's not a long-term

THE day Gordon Lee said 'goodbye' to players Stewart Barrowclough, Tommy Cassidy, Alan Gowling, Geoff Nulty and Irving Nattrass.

recipe for success at the turnstiles. All the same you had to admire Gordon for his guts, his dedication and his honesty. He did it his way.

One lingering effect of Lee's attitude in the transfer market was felt by Joe Harvey and myself a little later when we went up to Partick Thistle on a scouting mission. Partick's officials treated us to a load of abuse, which was staggering when you consider the reputation United have built up in Scotland over the years. The trouble was that Lee had welched on a deal for centre back Alan Hansen after everything had been set up. Joe had spotted Hansen and pressed United to go for him, Lee had checked the player out personally and agreed to the deal—and then phoned Partick the next day to say it was all off. Evidently he didn't like Scottish League players. Since then bad feeling had been building up and Partick had to get it off their chest so Joe and I copped the lot. It was understandable that they were annoyed but in the end the losers were Newcastle. Look at the success Hansen has been at Liverpool.

The manner of Lee's departure for Everton at the end of 1977 and the subsequent unpalatable display of power in support of coach Richard Dinnis left a scar on the club which is visible to this very day. The players threatened to request a mass transfer, even to strike, then ganged up to pose in front of the TV cameras and generally gave United the sort of national headlines they could well have done without. For a while the tail was wagging the dog. It was on this misplaced tidal wave of emotion that Dinnis was thrust first into the caretaker's job until the end of the season and then into the hot seat, albeit for such a short space of time that he almost didn't get his backside warm! Richard was a lovely man who was a rank amateur. He was completely out of his depth and inevitably drowned.

Make no mistake about it, United's return to Europe was due entirely to Lee. He collated his team against a lot of opposition and saw it rise to third place in the table by Christmas. All Dinnis did for the remainder of the season was not get in the way. Even

130

then United almost blew it, losing three games on the trot before clinching their UEFA Cup place with a 3–2 win over Aston Villa in their last home game. And thereby hangs a tale. Before the Villa match a director told me that Dinnis was to get the bullet. No question he said. Dinnis was finished. But what happened? United scraped a win, Dinnis raced out to hug his players who promptly hoisted him shoulder-high while a few kids invaded the pitch to join in the celebrations. Outcome: the directors witness it all and do a swift about-turn installing him as manager. If ever those characters felt they had appointed in haste and repented at leisure, this must have been the time.

Be that as it may, the inevitable happened. United started off the 1977–78 season with all the pace of a steamroller going uphill and, instead of European glory, we got relegation to the Second Division. United lost 10 Division One games in succession, which takes a bit of doing. There wasn't even a solitary draw to break the monotony and must be a club record I reckon. No team takes that sort of

disaster in its stride and United went on to lose at home to Millwall in the League Cup, before being outclassed by Bastia in the UEFA Cup.

This time there was no escape for Dinnis who throughout his brief reign had given a perfect imitation of a kamikaze pilot. His courage was frightening, and foolhardy. He repeatedly took on the directors over cash without knowing the full facts and ended up blabbing it all over the papers. Brian Clough might have got away with it while Nottingham Forest were winning the European Cup but Dinnis, never had a chance.

United, now in the throes of the players' revolt, decided they needed a troubleshooter to clear up the mess and there's not a bigger troubleshooter in football than Bill McGarry. So he got the job. I knew McGarry well before he arrived at St James's Park. In my last international against Denmark he was right-half to my outside-right. I found him a hard, aggressive, player, with outstanding ability in the air despite his lack of inches. As a manager McGarry had followed me to Ipswich and when the team won promotion, he publicly acknowledged the debt he owed me for giving the club a sound base upon which to build. He revelled in his hard-man tag, boasting that he was the most hated man in football but didn't give a damn as long as he was allowed to get on with the job.

In the short term he was a success at Newcastle. He cleaned out the trouble-makers, taught the players to keep quiet until they learned some responsibility in their utterings, and put a little respect and dignity back in the club. Having put the house in order, however, he couldn't create a team of quality. He over stayed his time.

Certainly he was given a fair crack at the whip, and in three years he almost beat the rap when, on New Year's Day 1980 United stood two points clear at the top of the Second Division having played Sunderland off the Park. But from then on McGarry's luck ran out. United hurtled down the table, and Sunderland travelled the other way to clinch promotion. After the opening games of the following season he was peddled.

McGarry failed badly in his transfer dealings. He bought badly far too often. His first two signings, for example, saw him bring Mike Larnach and Mark McGhee down from Scotland without having seen either of them play. It cost him £250,000 and while he recouped some of the money he never lived down

BILL McGARRY, deep in thought over the worries of management.

HIGH-jumping John McGrath, centre-half in the first team Joe Harvey built—the 1965 Second Division championship side.

133

JOHN TREWICK, a Geordie brought home from West Bromwich Albion for a record £250,000 by manager Arthur Cox.

134

those two deals.

Bill used to be a regular visitor to our house. His family chose to remain in Wolverhampton so he was alone in the North East and it was natural for him to seek the company of people he knew and trusted. He even tried to persuade me to return to football full-time, offering me a job as Youth Development Officer to Newcastle United. The story leaked out and, with my black-and-white background, I suppose there was a fair bit of mileage in it for my Press mates. For a couple of days I was severely tempted to rejoin the Club I love so much but I'm a home-loving fella, too, and when the TV cameras started setting up at the front door I knew it was time to cry 'halt'. I declined the offer with thanks.

Arthur Cox walked into St James's Park as McGarry's successor on September 4, 1980, strongly recommended by Joe Harvey. As Cox's chief scout and adviser, Joe made no bones about United's decline and he was brutally frank about the enormity of the task ahead. Things were as bad now, he told Cox, as when he, Joe, came back as boss to find the Club skint and in the Second Division doldrums. At that time United were around £100,000 in the red which is nearer a million by today's standards.

Cox still faces the mountain his mentor eventually climbed. His is a major rebuilding job needing three or four years during which he must try to recapture the interest of disillusioned fans at a time when the whole country is in a recession. It's certainly no job for the faint-hearted but luckily for the Club Arthur is a workaholic. His wife rarely sees him because he's out and about on Club business and when he is at home he's never off the phone. He burns with a will to make Newcastle United another Liverpool and that in itself is comforting.

Everyone with a black-and-white heart—players, ex-players and supporters alike—must wish him well in his efforts. Good luck, mate. Newcastle United means so much to every Geordie.

JIM ILEY, part of the famous Anderson-McGrath-Iley half-back line which won promotion. All three players are now managers in their own right.

ODD SHOTS

EIRE international Mick Martin with a hairbrush tucked down the back of his shorts.

ALAN SHOULDER reports for training on crutches.

DRESSED to kill. United's mascot captivates the young supporters.

CUP training at Seahouses and United centre-half Frank Brennan has a unique way of milking as he works the cow's tail.

HORSEPLAY—Joe Harvey, George Robledo, Jackie Milburn and Jack Fairbrother take a breather from training.

BANDING together on Cup training in Blackpool. Making a song and dance of things are Jackie Milburn (piano), Len White (vocals), Bobby Mitchell (clarinet), Bob Stokoe (saxophone), and Jimmy Scoular (trumpet).

JACKIE MILBURN and his wife Laura with an orchid named after the famous Newcastle centre-forward.